ALL THINGS RELATE

By the same author

The America Series:

Things of Concern- a Dissertation relating to the State of the World and the State of Mind

All Things Relate- A View of the U.S. Economy

Land of Opportunity- Opportunities and Guarantees in America

Ping-Pong (Rally's On- Relating to Pride of Self & Our Political Miasma

The Evolver Series:

Two Visions- Pathways in Nature Artwork-)with donna Jean Goldstein)

Look at Me- My Journey through Time and Experience-(a rather private diary)

Moments of Impact- My Personal Inquiry Relating to the Formation of Self

Conversatility- Conversations: Meanings within an Exchange

ALL THINGS RELATE

A View of the U.S. Economy

**Being Loose Musings
of the Author,
Churned to Concrete**

Joseph K. Goldstein

ISBN 10: 1478384689

ISBN 13: 978-1478384687

Library of Congress Control Number: 2012917483

Goldstein, Joseph K.,   1938-
All Things Relate/ Joseph K. Goldstein.- Edition 1.1   P. cm.
(Edition 1.1 adds discussion of corporate tax incentives, 5/7/2018)
    1.   Sociology-21st century-commentary
    2.   Politics-21st century-commentary
    3.   Economics-21st century-commentary

CreateSpace
North Charleston, SC

DEDICATION

To our founding fathers
Those people who, through their foresight, gave our country
the guidance it needed to become what it is
and
To all of us, its citizens, the people who live blessed in this
wonderful land of ours that offers us the opportunities to
prosper and attain any heights to which we aspire.

If I sound somewhat awe-struck by the thoughts above, I am just that. All my life I have lived in the United States of America, and never have I taken any of my freedoms for granted. Any democracy struggles as it wends its way into adulthood, and so all the trials and tribulations that its citizens go through are part of a process. Our process has offered us the best of everything, including the privilege of changing things if we wish.

In gratitude, I profess an immense thank you to everyone who supports our ability to stand on our own two feet and do so with pride of accomplishment.

Joe Goldstein

ALL THINGS RELATE

An Analysis of the Economy and Its Current Mess,
And Surprisingly, Some Solutions

Contents

IN THE BEGINNING

Everyone wants things to be better for themselves, that's axiomatic. "Better" is defined as getting more of what you want, whether what you want is good or not, at least it IS what you want. This has been an operating premise of my life- so long as I don't hurt anyone else by it, there is absolutely nothing wrong with this thought process, and by the way, if incidentally in the process others also benefit, that is good.

Right now, we are all suffering in the malaise and aftermath of the housing melt-down and its massive impact on not only this country, but the entire world as well. Of course there is more to it than just this, but a core issue is fiscal responsibility. So I have been spinning, because every time I try to figure out what should come next, I find myself in a circular logic situation- the old cart before the horse thing. But I think I've got it, by Jove, and I would like to offer my thoughts as a talking point for **a plan for our economy: to move forward, up, and away.**

First a look at the variables that have been major influences on the downturn of the US economy, as I see them (although not necessarily in any particular order): immigration policy, out-sourcing, jobs or "lacka", entitlements, oil-dependency, fiscal policy, domestic policy, taxes, cost of education, loans, values (family, neighborhood, work, political ethic), profit motive. There are more, but wouldn't you say that this is enough to bite off at this time?   Fear not, there is a common thread that will pull all these diversities together, as promised in the title "All Things Relate".
I do want to add that as I see a subject of direct relevance and begin a discourse, if at first it appears that I am diverting, I really hope that I have delved into the matter rather than diverted away from the main subject. Please bear with me; it

is not my intent to babble, but rather to offer supporting logic to a position.

So, let's start our conversation.

PERSPECTIVE

The thing I am thinking about now is "what's the point?" I mean, really, is there any reason to try to put together thoughts and personal logic into a publication that might get read by say, only two people, or <u>maybe</u> by a lot more, and rejected by perhaps 80% of the ones that get past the first few pages!! Well, I think yes, because it is cathartic for the writer, and I'll put that first because I know it's the only thing that I can say is true about the future of this book, and also because if I upset or get concurrence from anyone, then GOAL ACCOMPLISHED.

It's always good to understand the perspective of any conversation. In this case, it's one sided and one way---ME. So probably it is a good idea to get a handle on my background, my thought process, my beliefs, and my approach to problems and problem solving, because that is what this book is about and what it presents for reader entertainment.

Firstly, I have an engineering background, so I like to think that I am logical, analytical, rational, (hopefully not nerdy), and all the other things that make for good engineering. But in addition to that mind-set, established over 41 years in industry, I have two other sources that have been major influences on my life. One is middle-eastern philosophy and involves Buddhist teachings both Zen and Tibetan, plus the philosophy of Khrishnamurti through direct exposure to his lectures in Ojai and his publications after his death. The second is a series of lectures attended over a 6 year period, presented by Andrew J. Galambos, an astro-physicist turned socio-economist, who saw that although man has taken giant strides in medicine and physical science, he has taken only inch-steps in the field of human societal interaction, as witnessed by mankind's plethora of never-ending wars and struggles. His solution is recognition of property, both physical and intellectual, as a cornerstone of relationships (more to come on this subject).

So, armed with this triad of a background, I find myself looking at our state of existence in a state of appall-ment. How have we come so far but brought such baggage with us that we are at the brink of destruction? That is the world-view of my concern, and I have written about that in my book "Things of Concern". But here I want to focus on a sub-set issue, yet not less important, the turning-around necessary to get our country healthy, wealthy, and wise once again; for us to get our befuddled ways heading along a path that offers health, wealth, happiness, and pride of self to all of us.

You might notice that interspersed within the following heady text I have placed four sketches that I made as my wife and I traveled within California visiting some of nature's wonderful places. They are here because "all things do relate", and every once in a while it's good to stop and smell the flowers rather than the coffee. So when I get steamed up, I just take a deep breath and remember how wonderful our country is, and how blessed we are that we have all this beauty so freely accessible around us.

AN INTERLUDE- VISIT TO DONNER LAKE

(An appreciation of the wonder around us)

THE PROBLEM

In these United States, the immediate problem is a bottomed-out economy, one with much too high a level of unemployment, and how to turn that around. An ancillary problem; this country's spokespersons and implementers, the two major political parties, have drawn ideological lines that are so deep and entrenched that neither dares step outside their little box to get a bigger perspective, for fear of retaliation by even their own respective party machine.

The two sides can be defined by their primary positions- the Democrats looking at entitlements as a way of leveling life's playing field and thus giving everyone a little bit of everything, the Republicans looking at the financial mechanism and wanting to reward everyone who is on the road to doing well. Both approaches contain degrees of merit, but can simple compromise between the two (what the heck does that mean anyway) be a valid solution? It really takes going back to basic tenets, ground rules, and goals. I would like to start off with what I would consider the goals of the/any individual, because after all, society amazingly has a lot of those, they are the reason society is. I started out with the statement that each one of us wants things better for themselves. I'll stick with that as my first premise, and expand it by saying that what is stated as inalienable rights in the Declaration of Independence; "life, liberty, and the pursuit of happiness" are the triad that offers a "mission statement" and translates that statement into primary goals. To attain these goals, each person has to strive to his/her respective degree of being able to manage their activities so that they head in a direction of their choice. OK, we've got a start consisting of a focus on a problem, and a top level set of objectives, applicable to individuals and to the societies they shape. Everything starts with the individual in that everyone has intrinsic worth, and needs to apply that as part of their arsenal for achievement (of producing some form of reasonable life). The individual's intrinsic worth translates into an available commodity, something that can be exchanged for the least common denominator, which means barter, trade, or wage, and the result being the ability and wherewithal to pursue life effort towards happiness.

SUMMARY: At the risk of being (slightly) redundant, I think bulleting the main points of the problem is a wise move, since it places the issues in plain sight, not masked by rhetoric:

-Each of us has the inalienable right to life, liberty, and the pursuit of happiness
-A free enterprise system with insufficient guidelines allowed economic disaster
-Thus a resulting stagnated and depressed economy
-Excessive political ideological entrenchment is preventing solutions
-High unemployment is a result

Each of these bullets may sound a bit esoteric; however these are the items that exist as main issues in a timely snapshot of today's life and times in the United States of America.

WHAT DOES IT TAKE TO MAKE A PLAN??

From many years of working in aerospace engineering, especially system engineering, it is my considered opinion that one of the most important parts of any plan is the transition into it. There are several ways to get from "here to there": the first is direct and brutal and involves just doing it; another is to allow failure of the current system, thus requiring a move into the new; and the third (which I believe to be the most positively effective) is to plan a series of transition steps that eases away from the current and slowly substitutes the elements of the new. I would consider the latter to be the politic way to effect change, because it allows compromise as part of the transition, with the ability to tweak as things progress.

However, before such transition can even be considered, a first set of actions would be to logically present the conditions that need change, explain why change is both important and necessary, and what the change is all about. Perhaps just defining the necessity for the change is an answer to the biggest hurdle against inaction, since status quo and security are truly the lowest form of human happiness, and people are loath to move away from such a security blanket. And besides, quite a few people equate happiness with "lacka" responsibility, and so the necessity of moving from one position to another (thus requiring effort) becomes a major stumbling block associated with the embracing of responsibility. Impetus for movement may simply be lack of satisfaction, or the awareness that happiness has drifted away and been replaced by sluggish existence, or the intensity of being surrounded by a stifling atmosphere. Hey don't get me wrong, this is not convoluted thinking, because the motivating force for almost all people is self-satisfaction, and that is what must be appealed to.

So to start the planning process, first a mission statement must be generated. This is the grand view of what is desired, the overall reason for doing it, why it is important. Next, the objectives, which are the goals to be achieved. These translate into a set of requirements, which are the things necessary to be contained within the effort. Then the premises, which are the givens that must be worked with at the time. Also, an underlying critical aspect is the set of values with which the effort will be conducted (these are the rules of conduct, the morals associated with the doing- things that keep the doer on track), and finally- the actions to be implemented. All of these are the considerations against which the plan is drawn, again recognizing the necessity of developing a carefully crafted transition plan that will ease-in the change so that all parties/stake-holders can accept it. Let's just keep in mind all these factors that are necessities in the generation of any plan to resolve any problem.

SUMMARY: To prevent fumbling around and misguided direction, planning and transition into it are key elements of any activity.

TIDBITS- PIECES OF THE WHOLE

I feel that the first step of this examination is to look at the pieces that influence the problem, to at least present a background for consideration, so that as the elements begin to unfold, a matrix of commonality might appear. Each little tendril is part of a root source, each aspect offering just a gentle (or maybe not so gentle) nudge towards a path of resolution. But I have to say, economics is just another word for heavily-entwined, because clearly all things are so inter-related that unless balancing acts are performed, it would be easy to over-tip and start a downhill response to an uphill attempt.

In mathematics, one massively gigantic equation consisting of partial derivatives of all the influences would have to be assembled in order to truly time-slot any moment. That's why linear simplifications are made, so that holding everything else constant; you can look at sneak peeks of impacts. BUT the danger is in looking at some minimal impact and deciding it is too minor for consideration, and then taking that as an answer and moving on. Big picture viewpoints recognize that a little pain in several areas may be part of an overall winning plan. So here come the pieces, and then the synergies, and then the solutions.

THE ECONOMY AND JOBS

It seems to me that when you examine the current condition of the United States you find a society that has begun to run counter to its founding direction and against the basic threads of its history- a rather scary paradigm shift. Some portion of our citizenry feels a financial inequity. This is nothing new, but the difference now is that instead of rising to the challenge by trying to better oneself, there is now concentrated effort towards significant vocalization of this "plight" and **demands** for support and solution. This leads directly back to the concept of basic worth and translating that into life's tools for achievement. In order to live, everyone needs some form of "employable talent", some way of translating effort and justifying of self-worth. I put quotes around that because not all jobs or work are the same and are certainly not expected to be - you can own, run, or be other-wise employed by a company, you can invest and manage your fortune, you can take care of your home and children. Basically, it gets back to doing what you can do and offering that to the marketplace in exchange for your other needs. By the way, any and all of these "employable talents" offer satisfaction if you truly embrace them as a portion of your path towards achieving your own goal.

So we take our capabilities in hand and find a match between skills and market requirements. Talking about market requirements, we look at the needs of the free enterprise system which really means the needs of the society. These needs take two basic forms, one is the supply and demand of the marketplace under free enterprise, and the second is the assigned needs of the society which we can translate into government-supplied services. More about government definition will follow, but having government just create a job is not sufficient justification for it, nor is simply filling it- every work effort must be appreciated in some form of value received; and that means there has to be a real **demand** for this output. Marginal effort would typically be short-changed because it is not suitably competitive. By competitive I am talking about financially, urgently, or as a necessity. You might look at the agglomeration that makes up the supply side of the free market, which is populated by any producer of any product, here or abroad, and you will see that the producers product becomes competitive and therefore viable when someone (the user) finds this product to be suitable for the purpose intended and supports a satisfactory exchange (satisfaction in any form, such as barter or money, is the profit) between the users assets and the producer's desired profit. Thus is completed a transaction, a contract that results in satisfaction of the buyer and the seller, the user and the producer.

But as should be the dynamics of a free market, it sometimes becomes saturated with overabundance of product, when supply exceeds demand, when the marginal producer cannot sustain. The massive pullback in this country's economy is now just that situation, where producers are loath to get out there either into expanding their product line or for some, even entering the marketplace. That is because demand is stultified and unfortunately also marginally satisfied. Oh, don't get me wrong, lots of people want more, so demand is still there in the mind of the beholder; however, either the products are not mandatory or the competition is too stiff to support more product influx. Additionally, the idea of infusing an economy with make-work is simply a method of taking from Peter to pay Paul, it demands payment for service not requested, and pulls funds from necessary and productive use.   Yes sir, perhaps I've laid out some interesting and obvious groundwork for analyzing and solving the problems in the US economy. Ain't nothing new, but there it is, supply and demand- holy moly Batman.

To begin with, if we **premise and observe that the world marketplace is of finite size at any point in time**, then we have premised that competition is always stiff. So the unemployed, and the potential businesses to employ them, must fight an uphill battle to enter the marketplace. This uphill battle must be characterized by either uniqueness of product or of cost-value ratio. When you are up against a similar product at a certain price, you must rise to this characterization to become competitive. That's it, no two ways about it, either your product is appealing to the marketplace, or down you go. Sometimes there is an available work force and/or production system that operates at reduced production cost thus offering a way of competing by offering lower product pricing. One method of achieving this position is having a breakthrough manufacturing process resulting in reduced labor or material costs. A corollary is outsourcing to an area with a lower cost of living thus operating at a lower wage scale. If there is no out-sourcing, this interestingly could also be accomplished through use of a labor force that would accept lower real wages either simply as lower pay scale or (uh-oh) employers short-circuiting required fees and taxes and employees not paying required taxes. However, part of the consequences: in considering this, when employers pay low, the difference between this wage and nominal is the amount of <u>unearned</u> benefit that such an employee will take from an affluent society **if** the employee uses society's available services without supporting them. By the way, I am not talking about ukase-established minimum wage; I am talking about whatever deal is made between employer and employee. One might recognize that some jobs will be low paying, not paying what an employee might desire in order to satisfy all needs. People accepting these conditions always have choice between spending on necessities versus amenities, and if choosing **amenities**, they then might use some of the essential services offered by society as life-lines, and therefore end up taking advantage of such things as bottom line available emergency health service, food stamps, etc... without subscribing (by paying) into these services. Basically, something for nothing, but amazingly that is a reality if the employee has accepted the position with those unspoken conditions attached. AND that is why a free enterprise system which offers CHOICE on scope and content of services is a very attractive alternative. That way, you get what you want and what you pay for, and are not beholden to others, nor do you make demands on others.

A sub-element of the linkage between jobs and the economy is the company executive system. Leaders are chosen to lead, and supposedly to lead well. In the corporate marketplace huge compensation is offered as incentive to entice high level people. Huge compensation means salary, bonus, perks, and severance benefits.
As an aside- a friend of mine offered some astute thoughts on the current process and ways to entwine good performance with high compensation. In order to protect stockholders, corporations, and the economy; consider that any annual compensation above (say) $1 million could be put in an escrow account and dispersed to the executive 20% per year over 5 years. Any malfeasance, extremely poor decisions, etc... would cause the money in the account to head towards

zero, with no golden parachute. This would force leadership to focus on the long term. It would also decrease the chance that they would take huge risks or "cook the books" just to get the current year's monster bonus. This is all about the kind of practices which led to our housing/mortgage melt-down. Another sub-element of the linkage is the correlation between benefits now or later, and wages now. Here I am talking about the expense of providing insurance (such as health care insurance) and the expense of providing retirement benefits. I have no beef with these concepts, when you look at the competitive aspects you will see that the outsourced job has a different playing field and easily translates into lower wages, lower cost of labor. This will definitely be covered in another section, but it needs to rear its razor sharp edge at this point, because unless an economy is totally insular, comparison must and will be made, and not surprisingly, the economic weight of less cost will rise to the fore.

Stimulus acts, meant as methods of infusing money into the economy, are done through borrowing from future funds (bond issues) or placing new fees and taxes on today's wage-earners. Sure, this results in people working, and sure, this has productive output. But in addition to the discussion on whether the market place needs the products at that time, it must be recognized that we don't get something for nothing. As an example, the "American Jobs Act", a government stimulus infusion, spends $447 billion for 1.9 million jobs. Doing the math, this is $235000 per job, as compared to today's average private sector job paying $58000.
So where would the money come from to cover these equivalently over-inflated job positions? By the way, some of this excess is used for monitoring the program, thus creating even more un-necessary jobs. The plan is TAX HIKES, which means burden, as opposed to loop-hole closing and tax rate slashing which would allow job growth with plowed-back earnings. As for the sources of these tax hikes, how about: cellphone spectrum taxes that essentially make the user pay for the use of free air, reducing the itemized deduction ceiling which marginalizes home ownership, increasing taxation on

investment capital gains which penalizes wise investments, and reducing industry deductions on energy exploration which removes forward looking "incentivization"?
Perhaps it might make more sense to simplify today's tax code resulting in lesser taxation but more incentive for investment in the future by persons and corporations.

What is the big issue? Is it that rich people make more money now than they used to, OR that there are not enough jobs? Raising taxes on the wealthy (corporations or individuals) will not multiply jobs. Although it sounds good, "everyone getting a fair shot by playing by the **same** rules" is not appropriate because circumstances of each individual are different, and each of us moves into our economic positions because of capability and focusing on the benefits to be accrued. The job market must improve or no one gets a "fair shot". Our corporate tax rate is second highest in THE WORLD; flatter tax rates would promote investment and thus sponsor more hiring. As an example, look at the shovel ready Keystone XL pipeline which was ready to create jobs **now** but was shelved on technicality (a euphemism for political expediency). By the way, higher tax rates sponsor political crony-ism because lobbies will push for creating and obtaining countering benefits.

SUMMARY: Illegal activity puts the burden on everyone else. Comparisons of all options will always reduce to the lowest common denominator-competition.

Several problems now stated, and surprisingly, answers are available.

OUT-SOURCING, IMMIGRATION POLICY, and UNEMPLOYMENT BENEFITS

Many US producers see that the cost of labor in this country is pricing them out of the competitive market; foreign competition is producing a cheaper product. If the production process is not changed, then that may drive the US producer to either use the less expensive laborer (such as an illegal pay scale under the table at lower overall pay), OR outsourcing, thus using similarly less expensive labor as the foreign competitor. Of course, the offer of a lower wage or off-the books hiring of a citizen worker might conflict with either union activity monitoring, or falsely-established pride, or sometimes even the legal system.

To grab the bull by the horns, we **must** focus on reducing labor/production costs, so bear with me on the development of this theme. Let's start with taking a look at illegal labor-eliminating the illegal laborer puts many existing jobs on the market for the indigenous unemployed. <ins>**Illegal labor** comes in many forms, I will define it as labor that is paid a wage without having this recorded and reported.</ins> Now look at the unemployed worker who is either collecting unemployment insurance or is accepting welfare payments. Both of these entitlements were meant as a stop-gap, so that a person could retrench and chart a new course after stumbling. A positive program that starts by closing down illegal worker entry and illegal labor, and continues by penalizing use of illegals would open the door to jobs at least at that same wage, which could be filled by the entitlement recipient. Further, a system that forces all employers to assure legality of a worker, and then report wages as required, would support the overall system through required tax payments or fees, and result in less "out-of-work" subsidy. What it really does is cause all workers in any job to contribute to and support the operation of government and to support whatever entitlements accrue, while simultaneously reducing the need for crutches. Never mind that whatever people may make they will spend, the good news is that such wage earners now appropriately support and are entitled to valid government services, government being the central recipient of necessary income-related taxes. AMAZING, WHAT WOULD HAPPEN IS THAT THE ENTITLEMENT SYSTEM WOULD RECEIVE A FINANCIAL INFUSION AND SIMULTANEOUSLY

EXPERIENCE REDUCTION IN THE NUMBER OF RECIPIENTS.

To insure that this becomes a reality, employers would be subjected to a hefty fine for continuing the practice of paying under the table, and if the unemployed but employable would eventually no longer receive stop-gap or unnecessary benefits, this would guide and force them towards the newly available job openings. All of this on a sliding time scale that both clears the air for reportable jobs and gradually reduces and eliminates entitlements and subsidies, a scale that institutes a smooth transition.

(A word about transition- in all the efforts I have ever been involved with, it became clear that developing a transition plan from what was to what will be has been a make or break condition of so many projects and efforts.)

BUT, you say, this is not enough, some people will not accept a lower income, also there are more unemployed than there are replacement jobs. Good- now we must look at overseas outsourcing. Obviously, companies seeking outsourcing do so because their final product will be cheaper that way, and thus more competitive. Again, remember that I mentioned that US wages include several benefits such as health insurance which may not be covered in a lower standard-of-living country. This is where tax breaks come in for bringing work home, and penalties ensue for not (although this bears further discussion). This is not sufficient in itself, because the tax breaks will take time to generate increased production and sales to overcome the still inequitable wage disparity, but certainly an outsource penalty would be an incentive to re-examine corporate policy. Outsource penalties can come in many forms, direct penalty increment for not employing indigenous workers, tax breaks for so employing, and possibly tariffs that increase the cost of goods shipped in to the country. Ingenuity is a key, and although foreign competitors can copy or invent ingenious methodology, they still have to ship their products here; bearing the expense of an entire supply train and personnel, shipping insurance and paperwork, etc...and that is a pricing disadvantage. And oh by the way, as time results in growth of prosperity in the outsourced country, the country's standard of living increases and their labor wage edge dissipates. I have to say that parts of this line of reasoning, although valid, are disturbing to me because they interfere with free trade and the right to full products of your own labor, in that a person can no longer get the best and cheapest manufactured good at the lowest price. But, reality is transition, and these factors create the impetus for transition.

There is another factor that influences job availability, and that is automation. No doubt, with the increasing degree of automatic and programmable machines, and the complexity of such machines, there is a reduction of the number of hands-on jobs supplanted by these machines. But that in itself is not the factor of concern, because if the number of such jobs is simply eliminated by the machine as compared to what was years ago, that is just a fact of life and would be true whether the jobs are overseas or in-country. So the issue still remains that if work is out-sourced, either to foreign machines or foreign hands-on workers, then in-house labor is still not competitive. The challenge is to bring down the in-country costs of manufacture and then allow that to re-direct the work back here, no matter what the work mechanism.

So we still haven't got there, not by a long shot. Recognize that part of a living wage is the expense of living. When an economy is burdened with excessive entitlement, such as healthcare subsidy, food subsidy, education subsidy, rent subsidy, unemployment subsidy, you name the "-idy"; then the basic cost of living for everyone is increased; even those being subsidized will have to experience the greater cost of living. So that when 20% of the people require support from the remaining 80%, everyone's cost is higher, affluence is reduced. Remember that any basic minimum wage recognizes all these subsidies and sometimes receives COLAs (cost of living adjustments) as well, which is another reason why our products are less competitive in a world market. Too much of a person's salary goes out of control.

The focus must be placed on what generates excess in our cost of living. Not only all the "-idy's"; but for example, theft of any kind is a very real industry. Perhaps 5% of our GNP is associated with losses of that nature that are not recouped, and thus get spread throughout the economy. Further, a significant portion of our GNP is associated with our Armed Forces and our local law enforcement as well as criminal incarceration costs. These are functions that are necessary, but are as large as they are because of accepted need. Focusing on eliminating cause rather than beef-up would be a significant reduction in burden and a plus for affluence. And really, one of the worst is the concept of COLA, which caves in on trying to solve issues, but merely accepts the symptom and acquiesces to it.

We have to look at society and determine why things went wrong before, what went right or wrong with our implemented solutions, and how can we prevent negative recurrence. One of the lessons of our current financial crises should be a move to repair the legitimacy of the system. This includes assuring that the system would no longer be "gaming-prone", and that the persons involved in such actions should not be rewarded for their efforts.

SUMMARY: competition ain't an easy thing to overcome, and burdening with entitlements falsely inflates the disparity.

ON THE SUBJECT of ILLEGAL IMMIGRATION COSTS

There can be no question that there are at least two main issues associated with illegal immigration. The first is that illegal is illegal. This gets into an entire discussion about law and order, but especially the sovereignty of a nation. Is it OK to flaunt that very sovereignty not only by violating borders and laws, but then to demand services as well? In my first book, "Things of Concern", I address this subject on a broader perspective than simply the economy.

The second issue is the simple equation of in and out. The cost to the citizens of this country of allowing illegal residency to make claims on our society is obviously a burden. It is part of the reduction in affluence that this economy is experiencing. We are a moral society, so that looking at the illegally-resident humanity within our borders, we have acted compassionately, but that is treating a symptom, not addressing a cause. And so we need to come face to face with this specific subject, as part of the cause and definitely a part of the treatment for restoring our economy. I will break this down into several subjects:

-Supporting our government through the requirement to pay TAXES

-Drawing SERVICES from within the society which in reality are therefore subsidized by all citizens

-CONSIDERATIONS and consequences when dealing with this issue

TAXES

What are taxes all about? How about the method of providing funding for the approved services inherent in government charter? Holy smokeo- there are income taxes, service taxes, sales taxes, value-added taxes, use taxes, property taxes, you can almost name it and you got it. And how does one pay these taxes, remembering that they are not service fees paid at the time of service, but are "approved pre- or post-assessed dibs" on your money. Well in order for payment to be established and received, the payee must be identified and properly categorized. If you are **illegally** in-country, then ostensibly you have no proper formal identity within "the system", ergo you do not exist within the system and thus can operate below the radar.

Well, OK, this is not really the situation in all cases, because sales tax is paid on things purchased, and property taxes are paid even on rentals as part of the rent.

In the event that income tax essentials are required for a job, this imposes a requirement for either a SSN (social security number) or an ITIN (Individual Taxpayer ID Number, issued by the IRS). In the event of a false SSN it takes over two months for the IRS to identify such. In any event, even if social security is deducted, zero deduction would be an elective for income tax withheld. The use of the ITIN allows fraudulent additional child tax credits, (which amounted to over $4.2 Billion as reported in 2011).

Interestingly, based on the above logic, undocumented immigrants paid between $120B-$240B into the social security trust fund in 2007 alone, money they can never claim, but validation of the insidiousness of the method of entering the system at some minimal cost (social security tax), but not paying income tax.

SERVICES

In 1986, Congress passed the "US Emergency Medical Treatment and Active Labor Act", which states among other things that no hospital can refuse emergency medical needs due to citizenship, legal status, or ability to pay. Federally required benefits for which illegal immigrants are eligible include emergency medical and both elementary and secondary public education, although they are not eligible for social security or Medicare. Where the cost of illegal residency is most to taxpayers is mainly at the state and local level, such as prisons, law enforcement, child costs, schools (more facilities, teachers, bi-lingual education). Such immigration is a large portion of the national increase in public school costs-7% of the school population is undocumented immigrants, many requiring remedial language lessons. In fact, US born children of illegal immigrants cost roughly $30 billion, while undocumented child costs are $11.2 billion.

Being undocumented obviously places a burden on a person trying to get health insurance. 60% of those undocumented do not have health insurance, versus only 14% of US citizens. Undocumented illegals are 15% of the nation's 47 million uninsured.

Illegal households are 3.6% of the total population, but only 0.9% of the taxes and represent 1.4% of the costs. The net cost to the American taxpayer is over $20 billion per year.

STATUS CHANGE
A recent study showed that if amnesty were applied to the illegal population, the deficit relating to their cost on the economy would more than triple because of additional access to more government services. Interestingly, one of the main problems with using illegal labor is caused by our own minimum wage acts. It creates the illegal job market. But even if such workers had legal status, the American economy offers little opportunity for the low educated. Undocumented immigrants have depressed the lower-skill wages and prices for consumers. Employers pay 3-8% lower wages as well as less contribution to welfare and other non-wage costs such as unemployment insurance. Over 1/3 of the foreign born population in the US is undocumented.
One side consideration from reducing the illegal population would be that both dwellings and jobs would become available to the homeless and the jobless.

ENTITLEMENTS

An economy that allows individuals to determine their own needs, one that offers a competitive market for satisfying these needs would be centering on satisfying the basic tenets of the founders of this country. It would also be one that would reduce the need for entitlement, because we would begin seeing a synergy, wherein unnecessary entitlement is supplanted with a financial and competitive choice based on an income which is not encumbered by the need to support everyone else nor to pay for something not required by you. And where would a person's income come from? Why from the job now available because hiring is based on a proper common denominator of free market availability, and company formation and growth is based on a world-based competitive capability.

This must be traced even further back, really back to people deciding to have children, and recognizing that this requires responsibility, the responsibility to not only raise the child but to assure that the child has sufficient knowledge and skill to enter society with an offer of a commodity that will allow independent living. In other words, this country is founded on the spirit of enterprise, in which effort will lead to reward, recognizing also that the labor theory of value is false, that employment must be a means towards production for consumption, not simply that worth is proportional to work effort, but that someone wants the product. Not income redistribution, but income as a trade for value received.

All this because the concept of entitlement puts a major burden on the value of work output when a portion of it is drawn away (*without your consent)* for the benefit of others. I am not talking about charity, which is based on choice; that is a different subject, I speak of garnishing by ukase, the placing of a requirement on you that is not of your choosing.

Speaking of health-care, the concept of a mandate which must be supported by employers creates new fees on these employers WHICH THEN MUST BE PASSED ON TO

CONSUMERS. Since every employer would be so burdened, there would be no reason to contain costs.
This would be based on an overarching guideline that "YOU CANNOT AFFORD TO TAKE CARE OF YOURSELF". Rather, we could develop a system to accommodate the uninsured without burdening the state's employers and wage earners and consumers of society. Flexible individual choice and responsibility would allow cost-sharing through actuarial calculation rather than a free ride.

Moral Break-through: there are no such things as required entitlements. There is the working concept of charity, and that means from the heart of one to the stomach of another, but this must recognize what is to be provided, it should be only the sufficiency to allow the receiver to improve to the point where entitlement is no longer required. The impetus for the receiver to leave those ranks is that the available entitlement is life-sustaining subsidy ONLY, and offers absolutely no affluence to the receiver's life, only minimum sustainability. Somehow I cannot seem to say enough about the concept of entitlement. The free market has always looked at demands and availabilities and cycled through to create a balance. And that is what can and should happen in the case of anything needed or desired. The price adjusts as a form of barter, wherein "the pieces" combine to make some form of "the whole". When something is added, such as a stipend or a subsidy, all of a sudden the decoupling occurs and the value reduces compared to something else, anything else. So all of a sudden, the worth of products is reduced and the overall worth of the market is reduced. This is the source of the problem, the loss of value, the real loss of affluence; and the need for the ability to choose and value things on a strictly personal basis, weighing the worth to make the choices meaningful. It hurts to see things taken for granted, whether it is education or healthcare, handing this to someone is lessening its value as compared to a person having to select it from a list of needs, and pick it as one that has in fact more value than something lesser.

An interesting statistic: in 1962, 6% of Americans got Federal Entitlements; as of today, 35% get some form of Federal Entitlements.

Surface scratched, but still all the underlying questions and interactions need to be dealt with.

SUMMARY: you should get what you pay for; something for nothing is an "untrue-ism" and is part of a downward spiral.

SOCIAL SECURITY

(Never intended to be an entitlement, but now offered as a **benefit**, rather than a savings plan, so who knows what it really is???)

There is no question that our economy is captive to our desires to do well by our citizens. Social Security was originally established as a forced retirement-savings account for each individual. As such, it was premised to be an annuity, the principle placed in by a worker, the investing of this principle to be made by the government with suitable guidelines to assure promised payback capability. Recognizing that starting at an early working age and continuing on with payments until retirement, actuarially it was clear that the combination of accrued payment and interest would offer a tidy sum to the eventual retiree. In that regard, social security would be an annuity, but instead has turned out to be a voucher system in reverse. Social Security is one of those well-meaning but crutching items that was instituted to assure that the average citizen would not have to prepare for old age all by himself, that "big brother" would force savings and thus accrue enough to allow minimal existence when you no longer contributed to the work force. As time went on, it somehow seemed only fair that this forced savings plan should offer better and better benefits, after all, aren't our senior citizens worthy of it? But the problem is not worthiness, it is the old "in=out" situation. "In" was defined as a tax, "out" was re-defined as whatever seemed proper. And in that vein, the idea blossomed that with a continuously growing population, a "Ponzi" scheme would surely work. This form of the scheme looked at retirees vs. the work force, and at the time, saw that the ratio was perfectly satisfactory to support the system. And note, the political mind that conceived that solution would be typically in an income bracket without need of the social security "benefit", so who really cares.

And so, the concept of annuity, through extremely poor management, converted itself into the word BENEFIT. WHY BE UPSET? BECAUSE THE MONEY IS YOURS, AND WAS AND STILL IS BEING POORLY MANAGED, POORLY CONTROLLED, AND POORLY APPLIED. Well, as with all things, come-uppance came and we are rolling in it. There are more and more retirees, but not a proportionately larger work force. But, this is a big political football, because there are obviously pressure groups trying to maintain maximum benefit by spreading the deficit. This is part of what is causing our economic downturn; it is only one of many issues that have been passed on to future generations. However, when you look at the ledger, the financial community recognizes that the business of being the US government is rapidly accumulating too large a debt that will bite us in the proverbial butt soon enough, and the rating agencies know this. So what can be done with the social security system to curb its enthusiasm, just as is needed with any pension and retirement system?

There are four ways to improve the economics of the system:
    -Increase the tax on wages
    -Raise the retirement age
    -Eliminate cost of living increases
    -Reduce benefits
Each of these or some combination thereof offers methods of improvement. Each is worthy of discussion.

TAX INCREASE

A rather onerous methodology. This will definitely put more money into the system, but it is one of the very methods that has put us in a 12% social security tax requirement and still not put any lid on the problem. Raising the tax can be accomplished either by an increase to everyone, and/or raising the cut-off limit for the tax base, which is currently over $110,100. Well, sure this will do something, but what it is also doing is taking personal discretionary income off the worker's table, and giving it to the current retiree. Well, that is alright for assuring that the promise to the retiree is satisfied, but it is not alright for future generations. Remember, this method does not in any way curtail benefits. Depending upon the gradually implemented tax increase, the shortfall would be reduced, but again if benefits do not change, then this increase will eventually obviate itself.

RAISING THE RETIREMENT AGE

This alternative has some degree of shortfall, but certainly not significant. Today early retirement can start at 62, with full retirement at 66. Raising the retirement age could be established with a scale wherein those who are currently 60 or over still retire with full benefit at 66. What would be raised is full retirement benefit which would now occur at 70 years of age (as an example). This method, depending on the retirement age formula, could permanently reduce 40% of the shortfall.

COST OF LIVING ADJUSTMENT

One of my obvious favorites. Social security is now tied to the consumer price index. Solving the problem, or merely trying to bury the issue by addressing the symptom? This year alone, benefits increased by almost 4%. Dump COLA and attack the problem of living costs rising, as previously discussed.

BENEFIT REDUCTION

Initial benefits are calculated by looking at lifetime wages. By changing the lifetime wage formula to recognize some cap on wages, the benefits would be capped as well, and interestingly, would not affect lower income workers. Again, this would be transitioned into the formulas so that currently eligible people would be minimally affected, if at all.

Each of these options has an obvious impact on the economy, only the tax increase has a direct effect on the working person. The other options each affects up-coming retirees, but only gradually, and therefore allowing them to compensate before retirement. They do not affect current retirees. What this does is put the onus back on each individual to try and assure that they themselves take control of their future and do not pass the buck to the backs of future workers.

MEDICARE/HEALTHCARE

Medicare is a federal health program for seniors and for the disabled. Part A covers hospitalization, home health care, skilled nursing and hospice care. Part B covers outpatient hospitalization and physician services, Part D covers prescription drugs. Last year Medicare covered close to 50 million people, by 2030 the estimate for enrollment is over 80 million people. Today, Part "A", which covers hospitalization and such other services as nursing facilities, is calculated to run out of money by 2024.

MEDICARE and the "PATIENT PROTECTION & AFFORDABLE CARE ACT" (ACA)
The legislation currently dubbed "ObamaCare", which is ACA, has extremely far-reaching consequences. Its intent ostensibly, is to offer health coverage to uninsured citizens, whether they want it or not, and by the way, to levy a fine on those who do not subscribe. The plan also includes that any cuts applied in Medicare (seniors) will be used for total public and private rising costs for non-seniors. In that way, the plan was touted as being able to cover everyone at not an undue expense. After reviewing some aspects of this plan as

presented in the "National Center for Policy Analysis", report #330, <u>Medicare Trustees Reports 2010 and 2009...</u>, some aspects of the ACA plan should surely be discussed, especially with respect to Medicare:

-ACA will not slow the growth in health care spending as a percentage of the economy; it will however reduce the Medicare share.

-It requires cutting payments to health care providers for Medicare; this is how it reduces Medicare (part A and B) costs.

-With these ACA cuts, $53 TRILLION in UNFUNDED Federal obligation will be given "bankruptcy/wipe-out" status.

-Note that the existing "Sustainable Growth Rate" (SGR) system recommends reducing part B payments to physicians, but Congress has not enforced this for over 7 years (I wonder why?)

Some thoughts as to possible consequences:

-Constraining growth of Medicare reimbursements as ACA would do is projected to do as follows:

-today Medicare pays 80% of what private insurance pays

-in 2020, it will be 66%

-in 2050 it will be 50%

-Providers will eventually be unwilling to treat additional Medicare patients because they are losing money on each appointment, and may opt out of the system

-As a consequence, amenities and other services will be reduced, quality of care will reduce (less access, more time until appointments, more waiting time, less face time, multiple bed wings)

It is estimated that 14% of hospitals will be in the red by 2015, and 40% by 2050

-This may result in a two-tier system

-Seniors will get fewer amenities and lower quality care and therefore:

-Seniors may opt out of Medicare

-As a method for resolution, there could be a fixed "premium support sum" (a voucher system) for seniors, with adjustment for risk (such as chronic issues).

-Seniors can then purchase private coverage

-Future Medicare participants who also subscribe to private service would therefore pay more, but note that there will also be an increase in available delivery providers and plans which might offset this.

-In lieu of this pricing shortfall, perhaps top-down pricing should be eliminated, forget about one size fits all. Bottom up pricing would mean risk-adjusted funding; lower for some, higher for others, but proportionate to requirement.

-Then people could shop for a plan and pay with the premium support amount, therefore more providers would add both additional plans and competition.

Now look at the ACA, and see if any of the above logic applies. The first thing to look at is that once a single-payer approach is established, then all bets are off on controlling costs, or conversely assuring benefits. All this because of lack of competition in a free market setting. It is a joke to say that a free enterprise, private, for-profit company can compete with a tax-based, non-profitable, non-proprietary, non-incentive government run entitlement. This socialistic approach will only continue to raise its funding input as it deems necessary to minimally assuage the concerns of its constituency.

When I think about it, I realize that most entitlement programs seem to run into similar problems, and all fall within roughly the same options for resolution. In the case of Medicare, and especially in the case of the newly mandated ACA, similar to Social Security, these options include:

-funding increase through taxation or higher premiums,

-higher deductibles and increased co-pay

-raising the eligibility age

-reducing benefits.

-revised pricing structure

Of course, increasing efficiency of the system, cutting waste, and using economy of scale is always on the table. More to come later.

LOANS AND FISCAL RESPONSIBILITY

Let's take a look at the highly desirable concept of credit. Credit means borrowing, and borrowing requires a borrower and a lender. The concept of "consenting adults" relates to any transaction- "do it only after you have accepted both the terms and the consequences". On the part of the lenders, they have determined that for the reward of payback with interest, the class of buyer they deal with offers an acceptable risk for the reward. On the part of the buyer, they have recognized and accepted the long term obligation of continuing payback and the short term obligation that each and every payback payment is part of a timely obligation of funds. That doesn't just go for **our** personal loans, **our** car loans, **our** home loans, that also applies to **our** government (representing the interests of their citizenry) - when any of us signs up for a transaction, this is a commitment to satisfying the terms. Fiscal responsibility therefore requires a certain amount of brain-power, and if it is beyond the knowledge base of the potential borrower to figure it out by themselves, then hire a specialist, otherwise all you have is "false-fiscality", a word I just invented, and one that implies that it isn't based on reality and is not very trust-worthy. So when there is a sign-up, the intent must be to embrace the future actions required for the immediacy of a current situation, and to also recognize the history of prior commitments and the repercussions of any mistakes. Immediate cases in point are so numerous that it befuddles logic that they were not appreciated and understood. How about the great depression, the housing crisis, state budgets that have created severe cutbacks in services, a national debt that approaches 40% of the GNP, how about Spain, Greece, Italy, some of whom have as high a deficit repayment requirement as 130% GNP, and their plunges toward insolvency?

Getting back to the good old USA, the flag has been raised on the Social Security situation, it's been raised on the National Debt, it's been raised on the potential of Nationalized Health Care, it is recognized in the Policing (by our armed forces) of all the rest of the world, and it had been discussed before the housing meltdown. Fiscal irresponsibility has been running rampant, and the voices of reason were ignored. And guess what, the bail-out of the various large financial organizations certainly does not result in a positive lesson about cause and consequence. There is no question that top level management is responsible for their staffs, they either directed or concurred with their companies in their practices, or at the least failed to properly guide, and in consequence, such companies and culpable personnel should be required to reap their just rewards. Bail-out is the wrong consideration. However, there is nothing wrong with monetary infusion for a valued trade in commodity, such as interest in a company, but not by a government, because government should not be in the free-enterprise capitalistic business, government is simply a protector of citizen rights.

How low in the food chain culpability should go is certainly a valid question, but the decision makers and the knowing implementers are clearly culpable.

It is essential that the risk-reward concept remain part of our culture, it is that upon which our nation was founded, this means a recognition of "nothing ventured, nothing gained" with respect to the market place and with respect to life choices, as well as accepting responsibility for actions. So if something like a financial crisis ensues, whether on a personal or nationwide level, and if it is essential to satisfy it with an infusion of some type, there must be some form of balancing change to ensure that it doesn't happen again, that this infusion not be considered a reward or a viable outcome. It must be considered as a case study, with a very important object lesson.

SUMMARY: actions have equal and opposite reactions, so just rewards ensue.

COLA

I briefly touched on this disastrous concept (Cost of Living Adjustment). The problem source is that cost of living rises, not that we should get a simultaneous raise to satisfy it. Look at why cost of living rises, remembering that affluence is not the same thing as cost of living. Demand for more will logically increase the desire to spend, and if the funds are available to an individual, then a new strata opens. These funds should be the result of labor (physical or mental), and then are the just rewards of effort. Without useful effort being put in to generate value, the funds have impact but result in a decline in worth.

When no more effort is put into the generation of funds, then what the funds buy has less value. So COLA is its own worst enemy, it reduces the value of everything, and spreads throughout so that the entire economy is negatively affected, and eventually levels out lower compared to non-COLA economies.

COLA is a two headed beastie, it has a cause, and it is an effect. So let's get at the cause and recognize that when the value of labor (through such gimmickry as COLA) gets decoupled from the worth of the merchandise produced we end up with reduction in the value of the reward, which is now the result of the efforts of the have-nots and the "entitlementers" with their backwards logic methods of short term improvement spurring long term disaster.

Within a closed economy, if COLA were applied to everything, then **it** is worthless, because it has artificially inflated the cost of living rather than offering support to the recipient. In the competitive community, where COLA is a rarity, the consequences of COLA are apparent in the non-competitiveness of the products that are its result. How clearly can it be stated? John Arbuckle used to say, "You get what you pay for", and that is the bottom line, if you pay for a product produced under the auspices of COLA, you will pay more. Enough said?

Now let's see how that fits into "everything relates". Here we have companies trying to enter the market or stay competitive. Cost of production is one of the most critical of parameters, with cost of labor one of the major contributors to product cost. Clearly 5 % more wage for the same amount of work produced will increase the cost of the product. And the wage-earner is thrilled with the higher wage. But right around the corner is the competition, leaner and meaner and producing at bare-bottom cost. So the retailer and consumer buy the competitively priced product, and the COLA company sells less and has to reduce workforce. So some of the thrilled wage-earners are part of that reduction, and the cycle has completed UNSATISFACTORILY, because the symptom was supported and the cause was ignored.

SUMMARY: there is a cart and there is a horse, so don't confuse the problem with the symptom.

**SECOND INTERLUDE-
EL MATADOR BEACH**

ON THE CONCEPT OF POLICY

Policy is a flow-down mechanism, just as with any plan. It is like a mission statement plus all its pieces as it heads into the implementation phase. You have to take a look at top level stuff to really understand what is behind the actions; first you have to be sure of motivation. This is the part that really counts, because until you get to the driving roots of it, what you see is not necessarily what you get, it's only the current manifestation. For the purposes of this discussion, I'd like to examine two human interactions, the political and the personal, and get an understanding of the differences in motivation for each.

Politics deals with power interaction and power control. One of its purposes is certainly communication, but not necessarily complete understanding. It is the head-butting series of interactions which eventually result in some but not necessarily full degree of satisfaction. Politics is therefore a transaction rather than simply an interaction. There is a need for this form of communication because everyone has an agenda consisting of the necessary, the desirable, the neutral, the undesirable, and the abhorrent. Sometimes, the necessary falls into one of the other categories as well. Politics always deals with the necessary.

Personal interaction also has a degree of political entwinement, because everything I have said above is relevant. But it has another perspective, an emotional aspect. The emotional aspect is unique, in that each of us has a set of buttons that takes an external input and evokes both a physical as well as an emotional response. The emotions sit on one end of a spectrum, the intellect on the other, both offering motivation for action. Emotions are a powder keg, and will be triggered by perception, not necessarily by intellect. Different than the political, which runs through the intellectual side first.

And first and foremost about policy is that although you may be in the political realm, you are involving the personal, because when you deal with people, you are dealing with their emotions, their aspirations, their dreams, their futures; this whether it is punitive or rewarding in nature.
Policy formation always has an emotional component which may influence a political position.

FISCAL POLICY

What the heck, how can there be any question that if you can run your household and your life without going in over your head, that there is a method of running your government, which is simply a bigger house. A house, as an example, is a business that takes money to support and thence offers its benefits; and let's face it, government is a business as well (with a staff, a feedback loop, with goals, with income and outlay, even with a business plan).
Let's try some definition first, with the premise that we are talking about a democracy. Government by definition is an organizational entity created by the citizenry to protect the rights of the individual citizens. And according to the Declaration of Independence, these rights are based on "life, liberty, and pursuit of happiness". So then, the operations of government are intended to satisfy those multiple goals. Requirements flow-down necessarily follows. The various segments of the government, and the finances necessary to operate them, all must satisfy the basic query- do they meet the "protection of life, liberty, and the pursuit of happiness" requirement? (And by the way, it is not essential to exceed the minimums of that requirement). After all, why should something cost more than what is only necessary to satisfy the need, unless of course you are willing to pay for it? The rest of any monies or efforts should remain with the individual citizen, the source of the funds in the first place, thus allowing choice to the fund-generator. Of course, government **could** be expanded in scope and then it would be expanded in cost. Of course, it could then take on a life of its own and those involved in it could continue to grow it to satisfy more and

more, and more and more. Well, that seems to be the case, in that the definition of protection of rights has grown to mean the care and maintenance of its citizens as well, and the transfer of "what-that-is defined-as" has occurred so that the caretaker is becoming the caregiver.

This has become a major issue, because fiscal control cannot be established before charter control, and that has been lost, and most definitely must be found. Fatter and fatter, rolling on down the hill- this is part and parcel of the problem. When I worked in aerospace, this was called REQUIREMENTS CREEP, and was the downfall of many programs, and the cause of over-runs and schedule slippages on many more. In other words, poor management will result in being poorly managed. Major examination is absolutely necessary, in order to determine what is the correct level of entity to operate, and what level of control is required. Only then will come the procedures of the control mechanism.

Yet, there are some basics that are paramount to any form of fiscal responsibility, and they can be delineated even prior to the final definition of charter. First and foremost is the idea of a finite pool. Not water, but in this case, source income. This is part of a major synergy that always exists- unless specific balances are established, chaos will rear its ugly head. Once again, hence the title of this missive- it really does all relate. When you are big, you have bully pulpit and ability. For a while, you can move in an uncheck-mated fashion, you can swagger along living on reputation. But that creates and brings along baggage and eventually any house of cards will begin to totter due to inequity. That is what has happened, the state of borrowing from future generations masked as investment opportunity, masked by promises to pay, puts everyone out on a limb. The idea that "borrowing limits", established with the intent of securing responsibility, can continuously be raised betting on the come that everything will be alright, is a twisty messy path that can just as easily spiral down as up, and I mean in terms of real responsibility of action and accountability. The reasons are typically what were called "unk-unk's" in the engineering world- "unknown-unknowns", the very things that were totally unexpected and then must be dealt with.

And surprise, people outside the "creep-loop" will look askance at the teetering monolith and decide that such an economy is shaky and fiscally marginal, and that will reduce stature and effectiveness, vis-a-vie our current position in the world economy.

The real problem with some decision makers is time-lines; many of these decision makers are short-termers, while their remnant decisions do not go away as they become implemented. The trouble-making issues for which these decision makers must pass judgment are things typically above and beyond charter, because all the expected items are well-defined, only the over-reaching and establishment of new requirements raises and places responsibilities in jeopardy. This is "requirements creep", again something very well-known and always a condition resulting in over-run.

In recognition of fiscal policy, some of the basics of physics help put perspective on the approach. Equations look at two sides of a thing, simplistically one side can be said to represent the "in", the other side the "out". Balance is the key, and balance can be established at any selected time or time-frame. So the parameters of fiscal policy embrace "in/out/time". First of all, you have to start somewhere/sometime, and that should be at the time of the responsibility being accepted. Whatever the conditions at that time, they must be accepted as well. There is always one terrible "out" which is essentially immoral, and that is bankruptcy, the state of ignoring obligation and forcing recipients to accept less than what was obligated. I will not deal with that condition at this time, because it invokes moral dilemma and a cancerous consequence.

So let's start with the "in" side of the equation. In the fiscal world, that means revenue. And let's deal with government as the entity requiring this revenue. The governed have already agreed to a level of support for their government, and that started with the interpretation of our constitution to define the duties of the governmental bodies which require funding for operation. Governments do not (and should not) manufacture physical products, so funding is strictly for staffing and the purchase of products necessary for the staffs to operate. Remember protection of life, liberty, and the pursuit of happiness? That's the charter.

In the big picture, the US budget breaks down into three main sections: **Appropriated**- discretionary programs (such as security, education, energy) at roughly 35% of the total; **Mandatory** – which are social (such as Social Security, Medicare, Medicaid, TARP, other) at roughly 60% of the total; and **Interest** payments at roughly 5% of the total.

At this point in time, the income funding for all of these allocated budget items only satisfies **66%** of the total required. So where does this all make sense? Well, only in the minds of the time-oriented, in other words, let's borrow 34% of the money we need so that we can meet the allocations. And today, 2012, the budget requested is $3.8 trillion, just so that we get a real perspective. That's a lot of zeroes, and not surprisingly, is a big zero for those proposing such a budget given its inherent shortfall. The problem lies in the fact that for years and years the deficit has existed and been growing, and the cap on borrowing has consistently been raised to accommodate the budget requirements. Mercy me, what if I tried that, would it really work at all, would anyone be willing to loan me some money so that I could live beyond my means, with no obvious way to pay back the loan and its attendant interest, except the big ole "trust me"?

SUMMARY: stick with charter, don't embellish just because it seems like a nice thing to do.

DOMESTIC POLICY

Government, having been established as a protector of rights, and politics being the art of compromise, are often in some state of interpretive conflict. In its purest form, government merely needs to protect a citizen both internally within the country and externally from encroachment and attack. Politics is supposedly a way of properly exercising power through dealings between peoples and the recognition that opinions and priorities can differ but that equitability (hopefully) can be achieved. In order to move forward effectively, the least onerous deal should be the easiest to achieve.   Here's where you get the conundrum "given the choice, would you rather have a broken arm or a broken leg?" This question begs the issue that these both may be false alternatives, and anyway, who says they are the only choices?

Both government and politics relate to domestic and international policy, let's focus on domestic needs first. Our Constitution aims directly at domestic policy in discussing "the establishment of justice, insuring domestic tranquility, promoting the general welfare, and securing the blessings of liberty to ourselves and our posterity". Congress is given the power to implement by laying and collecting taxes, duties, imposts, and excises, to pay the debts and provide for the common defense and general welfare of the United States, with such duties, imposts, and excises uniform throughout the United States. All of this from the Constitution, WOW! Promoting the general welfare seems to be subject to swings in interpretation by our two major parties. It would seem that setting a low minimum standard would ensure some level of citizen welfare thus satisfying constitutional requirement, BUT don't forget one big HOWEVER.   The funds so referenced are to be spent on the general welfare, so first, what is the definition of general welfare, and nowhere is there a clear mahdate for the government to insert itself into the definition and implementation process, merely into the facilitating process. Follow that to the next level, and the question must arise about government sponsorship and competition in a private enterprise system. For government, protecting the rights of the citizenry should be ensuring the ability of the populace to make choices, but **not** to establish what those choices are, **nor** to implement its own government-run option, one based on funding from taxation or required fee, one that is built to run **counter** to the free enterprise system that is the basis of the country's economy.

One of the proper tasks of our government is to insure the various rights of its citizenry. Let us define citizen first. The 14th amendment states that all persons born or naturalized in the United States, and <u>subject to the jurisdiction thereof</u>, are citizens of the United States and of the state wherein they reside. That clearly means that the offspring of illegal aliens that satisfy the wording of this article, are citizens. That does not mean that under the law any <u>illegal</u> entity has any legal recognition, merely an identification as such, and subject to any resulting jurisprudence. Maybe we have to define a visitor status to those qualified, so they can raise their children. On the other hand, they flaunted the law of the land in the first place. Part of transition planning must recognize these situations, but prevent recurrence.

So again: a focus on eliminating non-productive requirements on our citizen life. Let's continue talking about social contracts. Is there a reason for our pool of community assets, such as funds for the needy, to be made available to any and all requestors? First, where do the funds come from? Taxation assures funding, forcing all those taxed to pay into the system, with the tax rate high enough so that those who can will be paying for those who can't. (Note that a charitable perspective would also make funds available.) An insurance system, which essentially is a by-choice investment, is also a method. A fee-for-service system also assures funding, but then there is the issue as to whether someone can afford to pay on an as-needed basis. Taxation is plunder, in that there is no choice. The remaining three are ethical and moral, because the products of your labor are yours for decision. But in any of these ways, funds fill coffers. In all cases though, the funds have contributors. Such contributors are therefore in a contract that assures that if they qualify and are in need, they will receive. Those that subscribe one-sidedly on the user end to such a contract are the ones who are not part of it; they are the takers without having agreed to the giving side of the contract.

Interesting thought- - do we have a government that would require health care for all citizens but does not require proof of citizenship? Is there something odd about this?

I have been following the race to the office of the presidency, and am appalled by some of the rhetoric. A simple statement by the incumbent sent chills up my spine- "subsidies provided to some industries are giveaways that belong to the people". What's wrong with this? Everything! In this set of circumstances, a subsidy is initially provided to allow an industry to get on its feet, to become competitive. In the process, the industry provides jobs, products, and profits that help position it in the world market. This is what America is about- the idea that competitive industry striving to achieve is a hallmark. The idea that this is subsidy and not worthwhile, and that rather than subsidy it should become a positive burden on industry and "given back to the people", is ludicrous. This is an investment, with payback. As a matter of fact, subsidy can therefore be defined as a loan and requiring collateral as assurance of repayment. "People" have not had anything taken away; in fact, the jobs created have been a positive stimulus. Punishment is not a reward. And what I see in that statement is inflammatory and punishing to industry and punishing to the free will and ideals of the American Dream.

SUMMARY: The scope of government must be limited to protection of life, liberty, and the equal opportunity of pursuit of happiness of its citizenry. Imposition of activity above that level puts unacceptable cost on the citizen.

FOREIGN POLICY

In this discussion, foreign policy must relate back to the costs and benefits to society of the way we conduct ourselves in the world arena. Once again, back to the Constitution for a framework under which we must perform. Here we look at establishing justice, providing for the common defense, promoting the general welfare, and securing the blessing of liberty to ourselves and our posterity. Common defense means focusing on the protection of citizen rights against externally generated conditions. Remember, unfortunately in this case, every penny spent is essentially non-productive in spite of the products produced- the personnel and weapons of war do a very important thing- they safeguard, but in themselves, do nothing to enhance the economy or society because their output is totally non-productive. But I must include synergistic benefits of research, technology, and physical production, and therefore must acknowledge that there is a major industry supporting the protective perspective. But for goodness sake, tilting windmills was a job for Don Quixote; and for a government, it is necessary to discriminate and decide what is a windmill and what is a real threat to the citizenry. The idea of any plan defining a program requires the development of goals and the establishment of actions to accomplish these goals. That means a big picture look at what the Constitution has defined as charter. Every complete plan must show its source and its cost, its stakeholders, its goals and actions, its timeline, and its expected results. In the course of implementation, changes will occur, but there needs to be a point of finale clearly articulated, and deserving of firm adherence.

The reason this discussion is occurring is that a major societal expenditure is allocated as a requirement for both defense and foreign interaction, thus reduced activity in these areas means less siphoning of productive output from the economy. There are also productive aspects to these subjects, because foreign interaction means conversation, and peaceful conversation leads to trade. Defense, unfortunately, is also a recognized requirement, because a strong capability means conducting business without being hampered by overbearing threat considerations.

In system engineering, a discipline I used when employed in the aerospace sector, there is a method of flowing down requirements to assure that a clear understanding exists before actions are assigned. Once again, "it all relates", and now an effort is required to firmly delineate scope and activity, and therefore the funding associated with both diplomatic missions and armed forces missions. So let me propose the top level set of requirements, from which personnel requirements can be established, and charter, mission, and activity can be ascertained.

Foreign Policy has one disciplinary goal- the establishment and maintenance of relations between national entities. This can be sub-categorized into peaceful goals and protective goals. It breaks down into three main tasks- diplomacy, trade, and protection of rights. All actions must fit suitably into a task category, or the acid test must obviate the action. Every logic train deals with levels within levels, thus rationalizations creep into the decision process. For each and every issue then, the threat or opportunity must be understood in terms of the bigger goal and sub-task, the niche must be appropriate, the actions to be taken must stay within manageable tasking, and the planned results must close the loop. This is not rocket science, it is unabridged logic.

Diplomacy- this is the crux of a world-view, it is the avenue that allows different cultures to mingle and for a world perspective of free interchange to be implemented. Diplomacy deals with both peaceful and threatening interactions. Diplomacy is in reality the ability to peacefully translate requirements into actions. It embraces the world of compromise, but at the other extreme it may utilize the force of threat. In our context, the idea of a contract is key, it is a deal that satisfies all parties, some even more than others, but at least it is a deal. The terms both obvious and buried within any contract are up to both parties to discover, equivocate, resolve, and eventually bind. The diplomat is required to fully understand the needs of the entity he represents, and to have the authority to modify as required to satisfy the end product. Good-will could be in the category of trade or of diplomacy, it is first established as a diplomatic objective, and then translated into the world of tangible goods whether as support of ideals or support of trade. Diplomacy is really a negotiation on a large scale.

By the way, diplomacy does not mean that the end justifies the means, rather that the end is the result of the transactions to accomplish.

Trade: what a wonderful opportunity for the market place. Here we have broadened our perspective to include all possible sources, in terms of making, buying, selling. Any deal is an OK deal so long as the parties involved are satisfied with the contract and it does not unknowingly adversely penalize third parties. Notice that trade means giving and taking, especially in goods, but as mentioned, also of good will. In terms of foreign policy, broader horizons are the result.

Protection of Rights: in this case, focusing on prevention of interference by an outside agency. Rights again are life, liberty, and the pursuit of happiness. So the threat against country looks not only at the physical, but at the nature of doing business and the assurance that there is not harm imposed. A fine line exists between self-interest and overstepping the boundary into imposition on another. It is the art of diplomacy as a first step in defining the boundaries recognizing the interests of the parties, and preventing unwanted imposition.

Why is all this being laid out? Because some degree of what is encompassed is required in order to bring the world into this conversation.

SUMMARY: every human interaction should benefit all parties concerned.

TAXES and FEES, WAGES and RETIREMENT

A government is the spokesperson for the collective citizenry, affirming and insuring citizen rights, goals, and desires. Government is a non-wealth-producing entity and as such, requires the financial support of its people in order to remain in existence. Obtaining this support comes through only two means- taxation or fees. Such things as borrowing through the creation of government bonds still requires payback funds obtained through either taxes or fees. In theory, the services offered through government are only those things required that are best defined by taking a national (if that is the scope) perspective; they include such diversities as citizen representation, postal, military, interstate issues, foreign relations.   It is essential to be wary of continued requirements creep that keeps expanding charter and easy expectation that the general populace can afford the taxes and fees to pay for the service. Life can be defined in many ways; one important aspect is to differentiate between "necessities" and "affluences". Our wages, earnings, and paychecks are the translation of our capabilities into a spendable commodity used to conduct and enhance our lives, and it is our choice whether to spend on necessity or affluence. If government begins imposition into our own personal selection of how to spend our money, then it forces our affluence level down because our real "necessities" by definition cannot by reduced- they are necessary to our life. If in order to cover these now newly government-established necessities imposed upon us, we must demand higher wages or, perish the thought, reduce our intake of real necessities, then we have hit a cycle which cannot be satisfied, that which will reduce the value of our wage because the non-increase in productivity for the increased demand on our wages places a zero worth on that increase.

As one focus, we need to re-examine some parts of our social/financial structure: the part dealing with retirement. For the longest time, large companies had based parts of employee benefits on the concept of the pension, which much like social security, was a way of accumulating for the future. In this case, pension funds were established and based on investment principles that intended to assure that Peter would pay Peter at the time of retirement. But, as with many plans, it went awry because safe-investment interest rates decreased, and bargaining positions continuously kept hiking up the promises. So now we see an interesting phenomenon in that benefits are a real and very large part of the job wage equation, and companies are forced into the position of either meeting the bargained position (and therefore equivalently paying higher wages) at a loss or having to try renegotiation to lower their costs and therefore the competitive prices of their commodities. The 401k is a partial answer because it allows the employee to place whatever is the desired amount into his/her own future. BUT, for the company and employee held to the original agreements, there is a conundrum that could put companies in non-competitive positions resulting in company failure and therefore no final benefit to the employee. Damage is lurking.

One possible solution based on grabbing the proverbial bull by the horns and reversing the situation before it becomes irreversible, would be the establishment of firm guarantee requirements and methods. This would involve the concept of insurance, preferably through private industry. First, each pension fund must use standard accounting practices rather than WAG estimates of the future to show current and expected financial health, thus suitably and conservatively projecting investment returns and discount rates on the debt. Second, the debt service on bonds must be met through re-examination of permanent caps on pension liabilities (such as retirement age increase, employee contribution increase, salaries set before retirement, and restructured health care within the pension). Third, new employees would go into a 401k, not pension programs. And fourth, then the insurer could issue tax-free pension protection bonds to cover the current underfunded programs- (this would require government concurrence, but recognize that the protection would only cover currently underfunded, not new programs). And, each projection would have to be based on solid accounting principles, not estimates, and certainly not disclaimers.

Taxes are an insidious methodology if not recognized as being a demand as well as a payment for service. An example is appropriate to illustrate the massive distribution of income that government taxes represent today:

The federal government is actually <u>spending</u> $34,000 per household, while only <u>collecting</u> $18,000 per household. The difference in budget deficit per household goes to future debt. On a per household basis, some of the largest portions of expenditure are:

> Social Security and Medicare get $10000, which is 33%
> Defense gets $6000, which is 20%
> Anti-poverty programs get $5000, which is 16%
> Interest on the federal debt is $1700, which is 5%.
>
> Most of the rest goes towards running the government functions. (Just as an aside, to pay off the national debt estimate just for 2020 would require $6000 per household. But do you know what, that isn't yet an unachievable possibility!!!)

Our debt ceiling has been used as a safety valve for the excesses of our government expenditures. This political year has been an interesting exercise in the difference between fiscal responsibility and political thinking. A bipartisan commission proposal of a $4 TRILLION debt reduction package was rejected- surely it could have been modified for acceptability prior to causing the credit of our nation to be put on the line. Both parties recognized that additional tax increases would be a known poison pill, yet that killed the plan when an additional $400 billion in tax increase was mandated during final sign-off negotiation on top of the $800 billion initially proposed.

The Simpson-Bowles Tax Reform contained provisions to lower tax rates and eliminate loopholes ($1 trillion available increase over 10 years). Raising revenue through tax reform would have eliminated credits, carve-outs and favored deductions. Raising tax rates on the other hand would result in economic growth slowdown by penalizing work, yet still leaving loopholes, and would not influence entitlements. Whatever happened to compromise and bi-partisanship?

SUMMARY: value-received is based on mutual concurrence.

ENERGY DEPENDENCY

Science has created one heck of a mess for us. Energy is plentiful, just not always easily accessible nor disposable. Our development in the physical sciences has created a dependence on its products, and puts us into a bootstrapped need for more and more energy as scientific breakthroughs occur. There are many energy choices, but as with all things, each brings along its own baggage as we endeavor to harness the sources. So long as there is a requirement for financial outlay, logic should dictate that the return be worth the expenditure. Again, we need to insure that this discussion stays on track, and looks at the inefficiencies of our processes in the concerted attempt to free us up from non-productive expenditures. We need to tie this discussion into revitalizing our economy, not to just putting together a philosophical discussion; maybe we can borrow and modify discussions already in process. NEAR-TERM or immediate is the operative term (no pun intended). That means shovel ready, boots on the ground, machinery in motion, etc.... in other words, things are ready to jump into the production phase. More of something already existing will satisfy the near-term needs. Recognizing that we are seriously attempting to improve our own economy, part of our focus should be leaning towards activity within our borders- oil, coal, wind, solar, nuclear, geo-thermal, wave energy- seven sources that meet all the criteria of availability associated with us doing our own work.

In addition to immediacy, there is a big and vocal portion of our population that is rightfully looking at eco-friendly activity. This current eco-friendly-**only** push, although having a long-term view, must be classified through using a short term mind set, in that as immediate activities are put in process, eco-friendly activity would rightly be placed in the planning and development phase, recognizing that research has already started pointing out direction. There is also the purer research phase that considers future concepts and sets up programs of exploration. Hopefully this helps in categorizing implementation time frames.   All three time frames require activity, from the mental gymnastics of research to the exploratory of prototyping of a design to the brawn of implementation and its perennial maintenance.

Boy have we an opportunity here. The high costs of energy today relate to supply and demand, but also note that many of the resources being used have out-of-country origin, and are out of our control. Beyond establishment of basic raw material price by a theoretically free market system, there is need for transportation from the oil field to the tanker, across the mighty ocean, into the local transport system, as well as the refining of the product. Bring it all home baby, that's one gigantic way of recognizing opportunity for developing both employment and self-sufficiency. Where we may have inadequate supply, that's part of the mighty transition planning phase to gradually bring it to our shores, as well as simultaneously developing the alternate sources. MR. PRESIDENT, SLAM THAT SHOVEL DOWN INTO OUR EARTH AND PUSH THAT DRILL DOWN INTO THE OCEAN SHORES. *And guess what, if the technology to do the job is there, believe me, so is the technology to safeguard against failures. But we must put that into the plan as a mandatory element.*

Some statistics that just came out indicate that the impact of trying to produce more oil within the US has marginal effect on market prices.   This is because oil is a global commodity and has many source locations and many consumers, and at this point the influence of US oil and its potential increase is still marginal at best. BUT, we need to truly generate a country-specific plan, one that looks at long-range energy requirements and either a superbly organized world source/marketplace, or antithetically, an insular one. We need short-term goals as well as long-term. And we need to craft a policy that has the staying power to be above political manipulation, one that has direct paths and off-roads that circle the wagons but still get us there, one that encircles the problem and shows a clear way to guaranteed solution. Less than that is folly and waste of time, effort, national will, and money, as well as potentially guiding us to disaster.

The big thing, the main goal, is to be able to offer our citizens a good economy, a good life, a good future- one teeming with opportunity to rise to everyone's level of happiness and satisfaction.

SUMMARY: energy makes the world go round. It is a dire responsibility to provide its availability

TARIFFS & TAX INCENTIVES

Tariffs are the bane of a free economy. Another word for tariff is inefficiency (oh my gosh, what have I said?), since it is set up as the lowest level of the playing field because it is absolutely not a value-added item and is reactive to competition, not proactive to meeting it. Tariffs clearly subtract value by representing an increase in a product's market place price, because in itself, the tariff is totally non-productive. It will reduce affluence, because it raises the price to the consumer, done so in the name of protectionism, not value-added. I am thoroughly opposed to tariffs in the free economy.

Interestingly, what I am recognizing is that today's economy is far from "free", it brings with it and has been shaped by recent events of nationalism and some of the baggage of socialism (which is the opposite end of the free marketplace), all as a consequence of political maneuvering.

Tariffs, and therefore restrictions, are a moral issue as well as an economic one. They interfere with the right to freely produce and market the product of your own labor. They contribute to scarcity by generating an output per unit of input that has been reduced by its application.

But fear not, as you will see, tariffs or at least the aspect relating to its logic, are and can become a tool, which if put to good use, offer a delaying tactic allowing a retrenching of position. So this is the context in which I will now discuss part of the transition plan to economic recovery.

First and foremost: a reiteration of my loathing of the tariff. Stifling trade is devastating to a free economy, and unfortunately begs retaliation from the "tarifee". However, refocusing this whole discussion, the central cause is really the need for reduction of excesses within the manufacturing process in order to create competitiveness and prevent blatant obstructionism.

One level of attack is therefore to look at the unlawful aspects of the current system, as it influences the cost of production and therefore the competitiveness of the US product on the world market. I zero in on what might be considered a secondary or even tertiary cause-the illegal workforce that slides below the recognition line and therefore does not contribute the "fee/tax" associated with the burden of running a government, yet in some cases, will compound the issue by drawing on the services available from the society. This is major, in that it burdens the legitimate society with the impact. Beyond the illegal workforce worker, aim must also be taken at the complicit employer, again some of whom do not register as entities and therefore fall below the recognition line. For the other employers, many ignore the lack of credentials of the employee, and neither draw from the employees wage nor pay their own portion of fees to the legally authorized government system of taxation. Remedying this shortfall will start a chain of reducing abuse of the entitlement systems we have in place today, thus reducing its drain on the overall system. Surely enough it will affect those employers and employees, yet in the same way as all others are affected. Effect of this action will be an eventual increase in the worth of the dollar and the worth of the worker, because all things are now accounted for and products are purchased, not given. Again, this reduces the illegal aspect of workers, and frees up job opportunity to the unemployed.

This will be a long cycle to move into the condition where unemployment numbers reduce, but as the value of our labor increases due to the increased efficiency, then we become more competitive. No tariff necessary, although the calculation needs to be made comparing the output of our workers and the output and quality of foreign labor, then re-examining the labor structure here for some reduction if necessary. Still bear in mind that quality of output must be recognized, as well as comparative worker benefits.

This is where some concept of outsourcing consideration needs to be introduced. A second level of attack is recognition of out-sourcing and developing the methods to properly compete against its attractiveness.
And here is where the tariff has utility. It is a stop-gap measure, one which allows retrenching, rethinking, revolution in approach. Plans take many forms, and as discussed, begin with problem recognition, then identifying solution, and in the middle generating a **transition strategy**. Can a tariff on foreign-made imports be used in a way which will increase the efficiency of the home made product to the point where the tariff can subsequently be removed? Transition planning is absolutely required, and a long term commitment to the final result. No hiding behind an artificial barrier, because then the barrier becomes a permanent requirement. Rather a firm plan put in place that improves the in-house situation and reduces the need for barriers.
There also needs to be a very careful look at tax incentives. Whereas the tariff penalizes imports by raising prices and therefore penalizing consumers, the concept of tax reduction is exactly the opposite, it gives benefit to in-country manufacturers by dropping their cost burden by the amount of tax reduction. It can be tied to companies bringing their out-source work into the country, or it could be utilized to simply cut local costs and therefore wholesale and retail pricing. Cutting taxes has a basic premise that the benefit to the producer will in fact be passed on to the consumer in a manner that makes the producers product competitive against out-sourced or foreign made products. It also assumes that increased volume will result in increased sales and revenue.

SUMMARY: look at where you are, and then develop the method for moving ahead, transition methods are temporary.

EDUCATION

Always something that belongs on every list. Whether it is education of the young mind towards a career, real-world application of a learned skill, or the honing of a mature mind towards recognizing challenges of the big picture, education is a tool that provides opportunity. It is a ladder that offers vistas as you climb. The human being starts with no natural instincts beyond preservation of its life and so we require learning, knowledge, and hopefully wisdom to become self-sufficient. How this knowledge is obtained and applied is part of our growth process, and is influenced by the environment offered by the culture within which a child is reared.

But education is not an end unto itself. Mind, being a repository where everything churns within, is certainly a reality for every student, and looking out at things through the eyes of knowledge is certainly an exciting benefit, and if that is all that is done with the knowledge, all well and good (although it hardly reaches full potential). Thus harnessing that knowledge and using it towards some upward climb of both the owner and the interfaces begins a blossoming process that offers a major return on investment. I guess I am suggesting that turning knowledge into a commodity is a good thing, and we miss a really good bet if we don't use all of our assets.

But this is a multi-pronged sword; propaganda and education walk a fine line together. Here is where cultural mores and moral principles within a society will definitely influence educational content. In a free society that allows open interaction between its citizens, it is important to allow such interaction to occur with no threat of interference. The basic tenets of human interaction need to be well established and freely practiced.   So what are these tenets, and how does a society assure that its citizenry has them available to follow? We get into one of my ardently supported themes- the idea of sacrosanct property.

In another book that I had published, I introduced the reader to the theory of "Volition" as developed by Andrew J. Galambos, a physicist who recognized that unless mankind got a handle on relationships between people, corporations, nations… that humankind was headed DOWN the slippery slope, not up. It required re-orientation of thinking to recognize that helping yourself is really a lot more than simply placing oneself first and foremost, it is also acknowledging that what benefits you can also benefit others, so long as there is no interference with free will and the property of others.   This theory introduces and explores pillars of educational foundation that are based on the concept of pride in self, and the development of self-sufficiency.

What I have dubbed education is not the same thing as book-learning. Book-learning is part of the procedural educational process, the formal by-rote aspects of transferring accumulations of knowledge. Properly presented it will help develop the thinking process and the preparation for introduction into society. What is most important though, is the development of a foundation for interaction, because we are an amalgam of thinkers, doers, empathizers, "emot-ers", feelers and anything else I have left out. That means we govern our reactions to stimuli in concert with our inner activators, and there are myriad drivers based on our hereditary and acquired characteristics, our developmental environment, our current environment—you get the picture? So deep down, our governing processes and reactions, very deeply embedded, are what direct our responses to stimuli. What gets drummed into us as we develop usually is given the strongest input because our young minds have very little defense against input. Here is where the real education belongs. Here is where the leverage is greatest, and I am thinking that if input is properly and strategically placed in a timely manner, there would be no need later to attempt any de-programming of any falsely held deep beliefs; there would in fact be only the most positive of elements.

How can anyone be sure that such things as truth and rationality are in fact what they say they are?   This is where a properly developed moral system of operation can prove itself and improve all of our interactions with others.

SOCIETAL CLASS: ON THE SUBJECT OF HORIZONS

Something of major importance is origin: social strata, entitlements, and broad vistas for everyone. But naiveté isn't really my thing, and I realize that moving up, whether socially or economically, faces some daunting challenges. I believe that any solutions to improving our economy must recognize that assistance might be required. This subject must be broken down into age related chronological time-phasing as well as goal orientation. The time-phasing goes along with education as a method of rising economically, and the goal orientation goes along with what type of education is embraced.

First and foremost is a basic tenet that the objective is to prepare for the ultimate goal of being able to live a happy and satisfactory life, one which has allowed your natural or acquired talents to translate into financial stability to live your happy life. So where does a young person get the opportunity and financing to enter this educational condition? First, parents have the obligation to raise the child they created. OK, this is easy to say, but too many children are the result of very little planning on the part of the parent(s). And, in many instances, the parent does not provide the guidance necessary for the child to move forward. Initial education through grade school is a part of the agreement between citizens and government that universal standards and availability will be provided and supported through the tax system. It is the job preparation portion, the personal choice regime, that needs further examination.

Part of any solution for the economy must include action on establishing methodology for job preparation financing. We have a system today, wherein loans, scholarships, and part-time employment are available. These three mechanisms are the staple triad that allows almost anyone to move forward so long as there is not severe excess baggage in the person's background. It seems to me that further embracing of the concepts by private enterprise would be in order to open the door for aspiring persons. This could mean apprenticeship, it could mean mentoring, or the promise to provide work effort at the completion of studies. Certainly industry could look ahead and see a suitable investment in the form of financing, and also receive incentives through tax considerations. This entire subject needs to be part of the big plan for economic resolution.

SUMMARY: proper education is paramount to achieve a suitable perspective

VOLITIONAL SCIENCE

One of the most important background topics that I include in this manuscript is a discussion and unfolding of the concept of "Volitional Science". I present it within this document because I feel that it has extremely powerful applicability towards solutions to the issues. As you read, you will notice the threads of this topic having appeared throughout. Of course I realize that I'm the guy creating this frequency of reference, but I find myself seeing it as a really revolutionary aspect of a "world-wide" perspective.

First some background: Volitional Science IS the interactions of men based on recognition of respect for property, (and by the way, ideas are property,) respect of interfaces, respect of individuals. I will start out by giving the utmost credit, appreciation, and understanding of the subject to its creator, Andrew J. Galambos. This teacher was by initial training, an astrophysicist who rather early in his life concluded that the relationships of man were postured such that in today's age of scientific advance, politics and the political mind could result in the destruction of the human race. Additionally, although man had progressed into the industrial era and was mastering the scientific, and man was moving towards understanding of the medical, the subject of personnel interaction between men, between groups, and amongst nations was still in a political mode that did not bode well for man's future. This gave birth to his concepts of property being applied to relationships, in a way that revolutionizes the way men view each other. The nature of the mind-set that would result, he called "Volitional Science", which was presented in an amazing series of lectures, and which is at this time available in his book "Sic Itur Ad Astra". I cannot overemphasize the impact Galambos' work and teachings have had on my life and my way of thinking. You might say "I am the weirdo I am" as a result of his lectures and material. And I must give credit to his lectures and the notes I took as being the source of much of my thought processes as presented below, of course synthesized and modified by my own life experiences since the time of my absorbing his ideas.

Some Definitions to Get It All Going

Volitional Science starts by defining **property** as a volitional beings life and all non-procreative derivatives thereof; (thus being just about everything)- that means physically, mentally, ideologically, whether part of you, or external- creations of individual action. This is the breakthrough- it defines **intellectual property** as your innovations, your actions, beliefs, intellectuality- orders of magnitude more encompassing than what a patent can provide, than what a dollar can buy. By the way, if you missed it, your word is your property as well.

Once you get this definition firmly in mind, then the antithesis is seen as **slavery**; the control of or seizing of another's property without his consent. A thief enslaves by causing you to give him your service... i.e....property, even if he shares what he steals with someone else!!!

Note that this has significant implications in the world of taxation. And **coercion** becomes the attempted and intentional interference with another's property. Note how this relates to terrorism.

These definitions begin the clarification of "right" actions. But, you ask, how do you know what is right? After all, you can now say that all disputes are over property, and then comes the question as to what is a standard for rightness in judging these disputes. First of all, how about stating that **rightness** is something independent of the observer; and has as a basis both truth (observability and repeatability) and validity (following the rules of logic). **"Right"** then becomes the "rational"; having true premises, a valid thought process, and valid conclusions. With rightness comes a basis for judgment, and for morality. So many times we look at the logic of a thing, and see it clearly a winner if **only** we could overlook some of the miniscule fine points as to whom it affects. So first let's look at what is **"good"**. It's actually a phenomenon of and by choice, so it's a relative value, quite subjective. Add to that the fact that if it pleases at least one person and does not involve coercion upon another, then it jumps from relative to absolute. **Morality** is the totality of all absolute good; it is moral if it does not conflict with the property of another.

The Key Question, the Universal Can Opener, is "Whose Property Is It?"

The concepts of men's various societies will be consistent with the nature of man, existing so that individuals can exchange property. Society is a construct designed to allow satisfaction of the goal of all human existence- happiness (a relative term) -all volitional beings live to pursue happiness. All concepts of happiness pursued through moral action are equally valid. Any increase in happiness derived through moral action can be called profit. Profit is not the result of a loss to someone else (that is plunder, and is obtained through immoral action), because one man's need does not represent a rightful demand on another.

Based on these definitions, there needs to be a bridge of recognition that profit-seeking mechanisms are superior to other alternatives. When we talk about profit, remember that any company, organization, or gathering is in business to make one, but recognize that due to competition, all these companies are at the mercy of the consumer thus being constrained to try and satisfy consumer need. And the consumer has freedom: to choose, to spend, to occupy his time, the complete control of his own property. That closes the loop, because choice and freedom are the societal conditions through which there is 100% control of your own property.

A major mantra of Volitional Science:
THERE IS NO SUCH THING AS A SMALL INTERFERENCE WITH PROPERTY.
The science of volition deals with the totality of the exchange of property. Capitalism is one societal structure whose mechanism is capable of protecting all forms of private property completely. Carrying it further, world government, the ultimate in societal structure, would embrace the capability of integrating overall property protection. All disputes are about property, and if we build a mechanism that both minimizes disputes and handles those that remain, we can eliminate acts of coercion.

Coercion has two faces: force (the tribal chief), and fraud (the witch doctor). Even in a democracy, both majority and also minority rule are controlling, hence the word "rule". Only in an economic democracy of the market place where the best product occurs at the lowest price, where profit is the moral increase in happiness, and failure is defined as no profit (don't forget, profit could mean increase in happiness, not just financial success), can we get to true choice. This goes beyond simply the buying and selling of goods, it involves ideas and systems as well.

Two big concepts form the basis of society-the first is the market concept- produce or be replaced. The second is the government concept- protection of property, a service with voluntary subscription for protection. Think about it, anyone can be elected to lead society if these two concepts are maintained because the market concept will assure the correct selection of people- if they are not effective, they will be replaced. This is different than the political concept-"there ought to be a law" as a way of governing- i.e.... the use of the gun and coercion.

So with these few inputs, the concept of Volitional Science evolves into a major human interactive dialogue. Key is the stimulation of curiosity, an essential in teaching. Note that I have not said training, the term is TEACHING. Training is not education, and agreement is not necessarily comprehension. Today's school system wants obedience-the goal of a student in the educational system should again be profit, in this case the acquisition of knowledge.

All of these definitions are snippets that begin to corral the concepts of Volitional Science. This is true education, starting out with a good set of definitions, one which, when accepted, lays the foundation for thorough and rigorous examination of the civilized world as it exists today.

Now To Get It All Going

Well, the above is a really quick and dirty overview of Volitional Science epistemology. Now the application and correlations to the various problems I have discussed. Start out with a new perspective. As soon as any and all property is viewed as belonging to someone, and that respect for property is a proper way to conduct one's business, then everything falls into place. When we recognize that destruction is an immoral act, and that the fight for ideas needs to happen on an intellectual level (at least at first in this our imperfect world), and that rational behavior is a right and conscionable way of conducting oneself, we have moved through what can be categorized as the "zero to one transition". That means that we move from nothing to something: before this event there was no baseline, no way for things to really move forward and work; and after that event, the dialogue to create more becomes a possibility. But this will not be easy, because education will require the breaking down and correction of the years of wrong learning; in effect, a de-programming of some very powerful but immoral thought processes. And you can bet that when I say this, it is with the recognition of Volitional Science as a baseline. That is how you can differentiate between that which is right and that which is not right, and the definitions are really pretty exacting, and repetitive, and rock solid.

That is why education becomes a lynchpin, and right education is the only way for mankind to rise to its level of capability. I believe that the methods of education involve significant repetition, first to get the idea across, second to get the idea thoroughly understood, and third to get it implemented. But this is not a "1-2-3" process, it is years of exploring, de-programming, rebuilding, rethinking, and practicing. And along the way, there have to be many dropouts, because this level of education is voluntary, and it is not for everyone's temperament and capabilities. This is where care must be taken in the structuring of the programs, because this must never become elitist, it absolutely belongs in the hearts and minds of each and every man, woman, and child.

Do you remember Aldous Huxley's "Island", in which the entire population, partially but not absolutely secluded, was exposed to and accepted an open, loving, and logical societal set of mores, and one which existed and functioned well for many years? It was invaded, overrun, and destroyed by non-societal persons with a dedication to the mundane and crass. Well, if you either read it or had heard about it, you can appreciate *everyone* embracing a consistent philosophy and attitude. No sense in starting something that a terrorist mentality can tear down strictly by the threat of destruction. That is why the principles of "Volitional Science" are inherent in sections of this book, because in truth these concepts should permeate everyone's consciousness as a way for us all to get along.

There certainly is an alternative, and that is that the technological advances would allow the isolation of those who do not embrace the philosophy. This is not to be considered as a dun, it is in fact a very logical possibility, in that if areas can be adequately isolated, especially by mutual choice, then isolation would work. Come back to that at another point in time.

Return To Some Basics

Take a look at Ayn Rand's writings, some of which include "The Fountainhead", "Atlas Shrugged", "The Virtue of Selfishness", "Capitalism", etc... She offers extremely intellectual and well-presented material that is powerful in that it lays an amazingly strong foundation for the "Volitional Science" package. This is not by chance, because Galambos' material is a next step parallel of Rand's ideas. As I re-read Ayn Rand, I felt the strongest confirmations of my own ideals and felt the strongest and deepest feelings that these ideas offer priceless guidance towards the development of a truly rational and thoroughly workable society of man.

Certain "Inalienable" Goodies

Saw a list on the internet, basically, interestingly, but not intentionally, an in-your-face version of parts of Volitional Science, which laid out a set of standards. The list was publicly available on the internet with an offer to share it with others, so I feel that I can paraphrase some of the items and use them in this section, because they so clearly lay out a mind-set. In addition, they are such powerful tools that these "values" must be ingrained within the mind-set of any actions planned from this presentation.

> -"You do not have a right to wealth. Get it legally if you can, but no guarantee.
> -You do not have the right not to be offended. In a society based on freedom, that means everyone has the freedom- not just you.
> -You do not have the right to be free from harm. If you fall off a ladder, be more careful; don't look to sue the ladder maker.
> -You have no right to free food, housing, or health care. Charity is fine if someone offers it, but you cannot take from anyone against their will.
> -You have no right to physically harm another.
> -You have no right to the possessions of others.

-You have no right to a job. If you have a tradable commodity, it is yours to use as you can negotiate.
-You have no right to happiness, only the right to pursue it."

SUMMARY: the philosophical methodology of "Volitional Science" offers a unique way of human interaction.

VALUES

Reason and logic aside, down to the depths of activity- never downplay motive, motivation, and the underpinnings that shape our activities. When looking at an action, you should always try to uncover the reason why it is being done. For example, the Democrats and Republicans square off against each other on the basis of party platform and published values. But most times in looking beyond the party in the major mind-set matrix of these totally dedicated zealots, one finds the idea of "ME". By definition- fueled (or is it fooled?) by the ostensive purity of a cause, zealots will march forward to an ideological drum beat that has them totally mesmerized. Of course, what is mesmerized is only the cerebral portion; on the side we find the impetus that supports the position. Keep tracing back and lo and behold, 99% (where did that come from?) of the people have a very personal ulterior motive, sometimes tied to jealousy or personal gain. So now comes the hard part, and interestingly enough, it grasps the personal gain part and can produce some very positive outputs. It has to do with concern for self, the "ME"!
I am not an altruist, rather I am a person who likes to think that this concern for self serves others as well, and that its origins tie back into a world view that produces pride in self and respect of others. It all ties into respect for property (which involves physical possessions, your own life direction, and your very personal ideas). That's all we've got folks, it is the sum total of ourselves, and is of a very precious nature, because it is the nature of our life on this planet. Now so far, this is an individual manifesto, but what is really needed is the ability to allow all us individuals to live and work together, and

that requires respect. HOW DO WE ALL RELATE? That is the real question, the real challenge, the answer to which is the real solution. We are all born with intrinsic worth, with the abilities to do something to stay alive, this is the translation of our inherent capabilities into tradable commodities that allow us to walk through the forest, wend our way along the byways, cross the intersections. When you look at society, you see an amalgam of individuals, each giving and taking, and hopefully doing so profitably.

It is pretty easy to take a cross-section of the needs of societal living and see that a plethora of skills is necessary to fulfill all the functions required. We are a plethora of individuals, and guess what, any and all the skills we have available can surely fill some niche requirement within society. That's the clue and the kernel of existence, we trade our skills for the opportunity to perform them, and in exchange, we get life sustenance and maybe even affluence. It is up to each individual to hone these skills and direct the action necessary to achieve the desired goals. SOMEONE ELSE'S NEEDS ARE NOT A REQUIREMENT ON YOUR LIFE, not unless that is what YOU decide.

Nowadays, there is a focus on what is termed the 99%, and that the rest should be paying their "fair share" or government will not have the funds to invest in education and innovation, etc... (And by the way, taxation increases on the rich would reduce this year's deficit from $1.30 trillion to $1.22 trillion. BFD!!) No question that education and innovation are part of the path to economic growth and opportunity. But take a look. The United States spends twice per capita on education than it did in 1970, with NO effect on test scores. That is not investment, it is mis-investment, and the solution must be more bang for the buck, not more bucks to be banged.

And when an administration points out that the causes of economic distress are globalization, high tech medicine, debt burden, housing bubble messes, aging populations, oh just about everything- time to back off, time to look at solutions, not finding blame. A big part of the issue is the $15 trillion debt and excess entitlements. Policy issues aggravating this include: the stimulus which adds $1 trillion to the national debt, health care entitlement which also introduces uncertainty into the economy, cap and trade which is killing energy initiatives, and ignoring the possibility of tax code changes.

I am going to take a chance here, and add something that has sprung up as a giant behemoth in this country recently. This is a political derivative that has manifested as **divisiveness**. I see it in every political speech, especially by the office of the president. What bothers me most is that the office is that of the President of the **Entire** United States of America, and that means majority, minority, and everyone else. What I see espoused is rhetoric of divide and conquer as the byword. Appeal to small special interest segments and force issues. Push and pass through logic, into emotion, and then into the equivalent of mob mentality. Offer a pittance, the carrot before the donkey, and immediate self-interest will over-ride the long term consideration. I am watching this happen, and it saddens me that such ploys and tricks are enough of a draw to overwhelm common sense in so many. OK, let's get down to it, bypass the rhetoric, and produce the concrete subject elements rather than the gross overview, although to be honest, the overview is what is critical, with the specifics simply examples of the danger. Worst of all is that the bully pulpit is used to divide, inflame, and polarize. The office of the president should never be one that is so small in mentality that it will override the law.

   -Immigration- itself a wonderful thing, but support of illegal immigration being exactly one of the situations that is eroding this country's moral fiber. Illegal immigrants do not have the rights of citizens, and the laws of the land must remain the governing criteria for behavior.
   -Taxation- you bet it is part of the necessity of establishing and running a government. The words "fair share" are part of the issue however. Simply taking through the concept of "there ought to be a law" is the very problem. Stifling the economy in the interest of leveling the citizenry is the antithesis of the founding of this country and against all economic principles of growth.

-Shelter- the idea that everyone deserves their own home is a misstatement. Everyone does deserve the right and privilege of purchasing a home if they have the wherewithal to activate that plan, but there are steps towards solvency that need to be taken first to qualify for that level. Before that time, other alternative housing arrangements are always available, that's what the free enterprise system assures. If there is a market, there is a seller, and that goes for apartments, condos, leases, rentals, purchases...... Bypassing sound financial considerations led to the housing crisis.

-Education- must be available. However, how much it costs is a market factor. Loans that can be either forgiven or defaulted are part of a cause that has increased education costs astronomically. That starts in grammar schools and goes all the way through graduate studies. And leveling the costs through government subsidy means everyone else pays, but what that does is take choice out of the hands of both student and taxpayer. And looking at the outcomes from many institutions, there are significant problems not being addressed, and simply glossed over in the race to the top.

I have stated just a few of the items that have been placed on political agendas. These things are all valid arenas for discussion and debate, but with decorum rather than vehemence. And that is the real issue, because when these and other items are politicized, they are brought out at a visceral level and tear consensus to shreds.

SUMMARY: do things morally and well and others will also profit.

Rock Buildings
at Joshua Tree
JCG

**THIRD INTERLUDE
- JOSHUA TREE**

INKLINGS OF AN ANSWER

If you have made it this far, you probably realize that I've been circling the wagons, picking out contributors towards a greater whole. When I started this discussion it was with the codicil that all the little pieces related and that everything had to be lassoed in order to bring it all together. And so we shall see that what seems like diversities are really similarities of cause and therefore offer the threads towards resolution.

The cornerstones are integrity, self-worth, and respect. How the heck did economic disaster ever end up relating to moral elements that (purportedly) offer resolution? Well, it's easy, because the central theme is "***sanctity of property***". What the heck am I talking about? How can that one simple phrase tie everything together and aim a giant arrow of solution into the midst of a world-wide crisis?

OK, now is the time to begin structuring that elusive plan that will bring every loose end into play and into action. First: a repeat of the problem. Bear in mind that although this has been the focus of the manuscript, it is a surface issue, the deepest aspect of the issue is entrenched in moral fiber.

FORMULATING:

THE PROBLEM:
"In these United States of America, the immediate problem is a bottomed-out economy, one with much too high a level of unemployment, and how to turn that around. Part and parcel with this problem is this country's spokespersons and implementers, the two major political parties, having drawn ideological lines that are so deep and entrenched that neither dares step outside their little box to get a bigger perspective, for fear of retaliation by even their own respective party machine."

THE PLAN:
(consisting of many parts and a structure for implementation):

MISSION STATEMENT:
The United States of America was founded on the grounds, perceptions, and premises that each individual has rights and can express them, and that these United States offer haven to allow its citizens to so operate. This country and its pillars of freedom are founded on the premise that each man's worth is an island of existence that links with others to produce a viable society based on the pride of the individual. **It is essential that these standards continue to be embraced in order to insure the sanctity of individual choice and destiny.**

OBJECTIVES:
For over 200 years, our society has been undergoing development and potential embracement of change; change is recognized as good as a result of growth. However, the codicil is that within the inherent nature of the transition should be a requirement to assure a positive result. At this time, the United States of America is extremely polarized by the attempts at movement into change, but the precepts upon which this country are founded are being challenged by these agents of change. **Focus must be placed on the development of clear standards for the future assurance of a positive aspect to this country's status and well-being.**

It is the purpose of this study effort to review the conditions of the economy, to establish primary causes of condition, and to develop a clear concise plan for not only guiding the recovery of the economy, but re-establishing basic principles of our society.

VALUES
We live in a limited democracy, based on the principles of a capitalistic free enterprise marketplace. These conditions are founded in the statements within the Declaration of Independence and the US Constitution. Free men have

freedom of choice, and property rights are a keynote to this freedom. All analysis within this study is based on supporting this statement.

PREMISES (conveniently repeated from an earlier section)

-You do not have the right **not** to be offended. In a society based on freedom, that means everyone has the freedom-not just you.

-You do not have the right to be free from harm. If you fall off a ladder, be more careful; don't look to sue the ladder maker.

-You do not have a right to wealth. Get it legally if you can, but no guarantee.

> You cannot multiply wealth by dividing it! You cannot legislate the poor into prosperity by legislating the wealthy out of prosperity.
>
> (When half of the people get the idea that they do not have to work because the other half is going to take care of them, and when the other half gets the idea that it does no good to work because somebody else is going to get what *they* work for, that is the beginning of the end of any nation.)

-You have no right to free food, housing, or health care. Charity is fine if someone offers it, but you cannot take from anyone against their will. (The government cannot give to anybody anything that the government does not first get from somebody else.)

-You have no right to physically harm another.

-You have no right to the possessions of others. What one person receives without working for, another person must work for without receiving.

-You have no right to a job. If you have a tradable commodity, it is yours to use as you can negotiate.

-You have no right to happiness, only the right to pursue it.

ACTIONS

The development of the action plan is based on all the above, it is the flow-down of a logically developed set of statements into the set of tasks necessary to bring the plan to fruition:

1. Prepare a clear review of the precepts that have established the nature of the United States of

America's society. To be used as a rudder to guide inquiry into change in a positive direction
2. Prepare a study recognizing the consequences of modifying the basic tenets of the society (modifying such tenets could result in a new face to the society, a new set of ground rules, and a complete overhaul of the mission statement and the objectives of the society)
3. Develop a matrix of alternative solutions based on the clear set of ground rules necessary to place constraints on the nature of proposed change to assure the retention of baseline pillars
4. Develop an implementation plan based on the selected solution
5. Develop a timeline and the tasking required to implement the plan
6. Prepare a program introducing and implementing the plan

COLLECTING MY RANTINGS INTO SUMMARY FORM

ISSUE SUMMARY (taken from each prior section)

The Problem: At the risk of being (slightly) redundant, I think bulleting the main points of the problem is a wise move, since it places the issues in plain sight, not masked by rhetoric, so here is a repeat:

-Each of us has the inalienable right to life, liberty, and the pursuit of happiness
-A free enterprise system with insufficient guidelines allowed economic disaster to occur
-Thus a resulting stagnated and depressed economy
-Excessive political ideological entrenchment is preventing solutions
-High unemployment is a result

A Plan: To prevent fumbling around and misguided direction, planning and transition are key elements of any activity. And most of all, anything like this manuscript must definitely go beyond complaining, into resolving.

The Economy: Illegal activity puts the burden on everyone else, and I mean more than just illegal aliens, I also mean actions that put other's property at risk. Comparisons of all options will always reduce to the lowest common denominator -competition. First level of investigation is to ferret out all the inefficiencies to allow for optimization, if that doesn't do it, then consider additional change.

Outsourcing, Illegal Immigration: competition ain't an easy thing to overcome, and burdening with entitlements falsely inflates the disparity. So again, look at what are the excessive burdens, and let's reduce or eliminate them.

Entitlements: you should get what you pay for, in the big picture something for nothing doesn't really happen and that illusion has created a downward spiral. Choice is critical, both to the giver and the receiver.

Loans and Fiscal Responsibility: actions have equal and opposite reactions, therefore "just rewards" ensue. This has to do with a person's word, with the moral standards of a person's life. It is a direct external reflection of their internal mechanisms.

COLA: there is a cart and there is a horse, so don't confuse the problem with the symptom. This is a "poor me" approach. **"OF COURSE"**, everyone always deserves more.

Fiscal Policy: to those entrusted with it, stick with charter, don't embellish just because it seems like a nice thing to do. Take a proprietary interest. Requirements creep can be creepy, and "earmarks" should forever be dunned.

Domestic Policy: The scope of government is defined as limited to protection of life, liberty, and the equal opportunity of pursuit of happiness of its citizenry. Imposition of activity above that level puts added cost on the citizen.

Foreign Policy: every human interaction should benefit all parties concerned. Expanding the scope of our awareness is good, and we need to be aware of differences.

Taxes: value-received is based on mutual concurrence. You could call it taxation, but the reality is that when it spreads in scope it becomes plunder; unless the big behemoth is well contained, it can grow into excess.

Energy Dependency: energy makes the world go round. It is a tremendous responsibility to provide and assure its availability, and what the heck, through free enterprise, the best competitor will out in the end.

Tariffs: look at where you are, and then develop the method for moving ahead, transition methods are temporary. So long as it is definitely used for transition only, the tariff does offer an opportunity for partial isolation, recovery, and subsequent revolution (turning around).

Education: proper education is paramount to achieving a suitable perspective. Today, the first thing necessary is de-programming of standards that are the antithesis of this country's manifest destiny.

Volitional Science: the philosophical methodology of "Volitional Science" offers a unique way for human interaction, an opportunity to excel based on each individual's merits.

Values: do things morally and well and others will also profit.

Please forgive my rambling methodology, everything is part of the building blocks that get there, and the necessary path is the one that lets logic have free reign so that when it is all done, it can withstand the challenge of criticism.
I find that creating a mind-map or flow chart, a grouping of subjects, thoughts, events, etc… that eventually must relate, is a nice way of pulling all the elements out into the open for viewing and then supports the process of organizing them. Bear in mind that I have not tried to solve all the problems of the world, but simply put together some elements that I feel relate to issues with the US economy and perhaps a bigger perspective that covers a deeper shortfall. So I have created the following flow chart that tries to connect and inter-relate some of the elements. (Sure looks like a bit of everything).

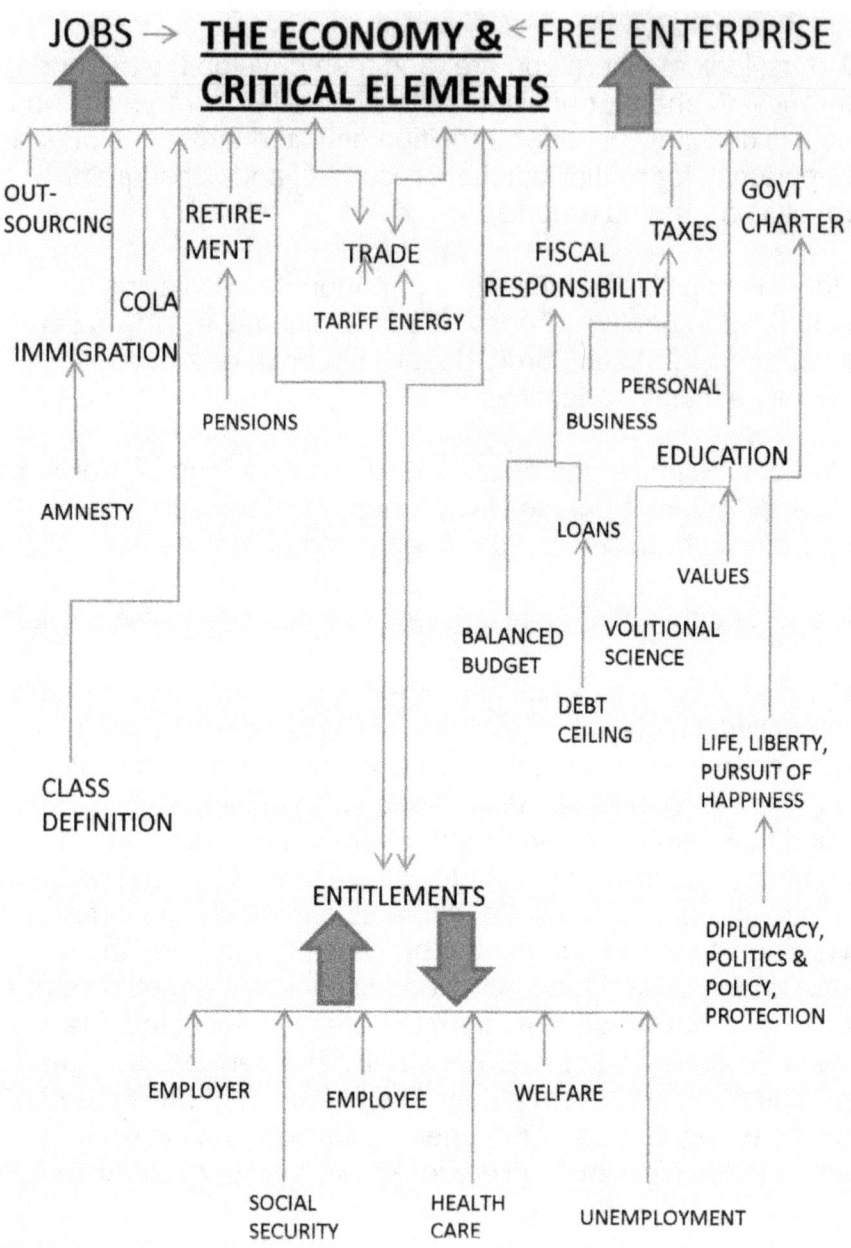

The flow chart may seem like a confusing array of items and arrows, and even defying logic as to what and why. But, from this effort and based on the previous text, will come a set of actions that would be great contributors towards solutions. This; especially when you look again at the issues summary.

Inherent is promoting free market concepts and transactions- the pillars are delineated below, and are the pieces upon which society should be built.

-The concept of insurance can be applied to every transaction, even investments. What this does is allow the free market to cover all bets.
-The concept of personal responsibility must be ingrained into all interactions, involving the use of insurance as a subscribed-to backup in lieu of punitive measures. (Guidelines for such interactions can be borrowed from "The Four Agreements" by Ruiz

Your WORD must be impeccable
Do not take events personally
Never assume
Try, and do your very best in all endeavors)
-Assure that transition planning is smooth
All transitions should work on a time-related scale, with time frame related to impact.
For each time slot in any plan's program schedule, suitable tasking is necessary to accomplish the professed result.
-Balance is part of nature. OUT=IN, where in this case the equal sign is a **MUST**.
When income reduces, outlay **must** reduce
-Government must transfer tasking wherever possible to the private sector, and simply stick with those items under direct charter. This will reduce taxes and replace them with a by-choice fee for service (not necessarily proportional to income), but definitely one of your own choosing.

-Separate and firewall any accounts associated with entitlements, with visible and tangible validation that output is proportional to input and is relevant to the issue under the entitlement. (Guess what- a large pension means a large contribution.)

WELL, HERE WE GO

FORMULATION:

ACTION 1 –REVIEW OF THE FOUNDING PRECEPTS

The basis of our country's culture is respect for the law, and the law has as its base both the "Declaration of Independence" and the "US Constitution". Key to both of these is respect for property, both physical and intellectual; the protection of such property rights has allowed US society to flourish because in all instances; personal blood, sweat, and tears have always translated into personal tangible results. Partial success, and even failure, has been acceptable (hopefully as an interim condition only), because our society has been tolerant and commends effort put forth towards achievement. The real key has been respect for the law of the land, allowing freedom of choice.
In regards to leadership, paraphrasing words in the Federalist Papers, interestingly history has shown that "expressed concern for the rights of the people", rather than "vigor in assuring the adequacy of government", has been a much more certain road to the introduction of **despotism**, and that of those men who have overturned the liberties of republics, the greatest number have begun their career by paying an obsequious court to the people; commencing (as) demagogues, and ending (as) tyrants. Why would I bring up this set of information? Look at what is going on today.

Therefore, I will not spend time on discussing history, rather I would look at what we have now and trace back philosophically to what were the foundations at the start.

Today's United States is an interesting amalgam with appeal to all sorts of people who want to do well. As previously noted, doing well is a relative statement, because some people wish to excel, while others strive to simply get along. There is a major difference in goals and mind-set between these two groups, and within them are sub-sets. To excel means simply to stand-out, to surpass, to outdo. There are no moral prerogatives within that definition, and yet, one can see a spectrum relating to respect for the law. This is where acknowledgement must be given to two driving elements. The first is the impetus to excel, the second is that when a society is embraced, its rules are also embraced, and violations of these rules should rightly invoke dunning. So this allows that the dichotomy can exist and will follow the concept of respect for property, respect for the law.

ACTION 2 –TENETS OF SOCIETY

What needs to be done for this action is to look at possible changes in overall society as a result of adopting new sets of ground rules. Once the underlying tenets change, then the entire mission statement, the personal interactions, the goals, the very nature of living within the society will go through revolution. First-where were we?

Putting a focus on the nature of the people that populated the early United States is pretty easy to do. Except for Native Americans, everyone was an immigrant. Most Native American cultures were based on the pride of the individual, most were hunters whose existence depended on the translation of their capabilities into methods of dealing with nature. Banding together was for mutual self-preservation, for protection against the elements and against enemies. Most parts of the United States are in the temperate zone, and so elements of the four seasons imposed themselves on the people and where seasonal changes occurred, the populace was the stronger for adapting.

Immigrants and colonists came to this country with two major goals- the search for freedom of religion, and improvement of quality of life, taken in form of economics and intellectualism. Nothing was a given, everything was an uphill battle to achieve. Many immigrants came with very little except expectation and will.

And so the foundations of our country were based on the struggle to exist and to rise, and the mettle of the early inhabitants was one of accepting this challenge. The building blocks of our culture have always been those of improvement. Whether it is school matriculation, or worker promotion, or getting married, each has done its share towards creating a "growing" environment.

Well, what if we begin the process of challenging and eliminating the very cornerstones of our culture and our society, and consider replacing them with less challenging, less individualistic, less pride-generating concepts (although I will acknowledge that some people will look with pride upon a socialistic system)?

So let's start this awful exercise by corralling and then dropping the basics of the US Constitution- no more guarantee of life, liberty, and the pursuit of individual happiness. Instead, let's simply premise the goal of guaranteed minimums in every facet of our life, in everything we do, for everything we want. Let's see- we need to establish what encompasses every facet of our lives, we need to have a group of experts for each facet that can ukase what aspects lie within the charter, and what minimums need to be prescribed. Once the committees are formed for determining charter, rules, and requirements, we need to establish who can satisfactorily be qualified as implementers of policy, who will judge as to whether claims are qualified, and who will police the activity to ensure everyone gets to use it, use it fairly, and who abides by the rules.

Oh-my-gosh, I think I just established mini-governments for each of the cherished entitlements, let's see- we will need a legislative branch to make the rules, a judicial branch to make sure everyone is performing according to the rules, and an executive branch to make sure it is done right and to catch the non-compliers. And we would need each of these bureaucracies for each and every facet. But that's only the tip of the proverbial "iceberg". Because this is no longer free enterprise, but rather "freely available", we need to look at how this will be financed. Well, we know that if everyone MUST subscribe, then everyone MUST contribute. Not choice in terms of "will you: rather you **must**". And you will get the minimum, that's a promise.

What are these cherished entitlements? As I premised, every facet of your life will be subject to these minimum requirements. You eat, well then you and everyone else will get staple minimums- never mind if you want to splurge a little, that is beyond your minimum!! You need shelter, well then let's get you into affordable housing, and for a family of three you will get two bedrooms, a common room (not family room, not living room), a kitchen with a little bit of space for an eating table and chairs, one bathroom with a bathtub. Shame on you for asking about a pool, about parking space, about a small outside area with a lawn. You need clothing; well there is an established template for each climate zone. You need health care-anything you could imagine is available, and we will assure that there are hospitals, doctors, equipment available on a momentary notice (or maybe not momentary because things are getting expensive as everyone avails themselves of the "free care" as desired). Oh, wait a minute; you need to arbitrate with your judicial group whether or not your case is urgent, or even covered!

Hey, what about retirement? We all get it, and we'll pass the bucks around so that even those who didn't think ahead can feel comfortable with taking from everyone else. Let me simply suggest that if you have too much of something, you really should be sharing it with someone else; you needn't even know who will benefit from your hard labor. Bottom line, a society wherein you are made to feel guilty if you strive to get ahead, where you are made to feel guilty for having more and not giving it away.

How to pay for these wonderful blessings? Don't worry, if you want it, someone else will pay for it, and not only that, if we are out of funds, either we reduce the payment or we pass it on with a future bond that will catch your kids later.

I don't know if you have noticed, but the mentality of U-Owe-Me is at work here, and frankly, I don't particularly like it. Don't worry, income re-distribution solves all. Except that those who work hard and look towards their future now have no incentive to do so later. Search around for a way out, and that loop-hole will be closed by the ever-present charter group (the legislature of this particular facet). And don't forget, each facet will be jealously guarding their territory against infringement by any other that wants to re-distribute your basic worth. Almost smacks of proprietary interest, Holy Hannah.

Do I sound a bit biased? I hope so, because all of a sudden the very incentive to excel has been squashed and flattened. Who will want to come here to live except those who want to take and those who are happy at the lowest form of existence where benefit exceeds effort? Who will live here but a bunch of takers? I have deliberately developed a worst case scenario, and this was done because once the first step is taken, the floodgates open and "incrementalism" insidiously moves forward until it blossoms as a full-fledged adult. It is a scenario that has been historically proven in all human civilizations.

ACTION 3- MATRIX OF ALTERNATIVES

I will examine only three alternatives; 1-RESTORATION to a free enterprise, capitalistic structure, 2-AS WE ARE TODAY-a mixed bag, or 3-moving into SOCIALISM. It will be done as a classical system engineering trade-off matrix, one that looks at cost, performance, schedule, supportability, and risk. These factors are a way of stepping back and dropping emotion out of the equation and simply placing the facts out for full consideration.

First comes defining the systems under discussion.

RESTORATION: I call this definition Restoration, but in reality it is more Return to Basics, even more-"Flaming Capitalism". Perhaps I am a bit melodramatic, or perhaps idealistic, but to me the key is always property. That is the one thing about the US that just radiates, the idea that what you earn is truly yours. The trade is clear, what I've got is mine and I will willingly negotiate what is mine in trade for what I either desire or need. Notice I have added desire, because although I may desire something, it is my choice to obtain it or not, in exchange for whatever portion of what I have that I am willing to offer. That means that if I want to say no, that is my privilege and must be supported by our societal system's laws. This immediately gets into the subject of entitlements, because in our free society, there has always been choice as to whether you accept something or not. Our government has the charter to assure funding to run said government, and that goes along with the idea of what elected government is all about. So the idea of entitlements is an alien concept to this country, forcing payment to support re-distribution of wealth, sending that money into things that are given rather than selected is against the grain of the concept of the country. I am also talking about the competitive market, and allowing it to flourish and fluctuate in response to natural market demands, without government interference or competition.

AS-WE-ARE-TODAY: We have surely drifted from original intent. At this moment, we stand on a brink, because there is a slow entrenchment that is bringing us ever closer to a big brother society. Let's take a look at what we have in terms of degree of nanny-ism.

Perhaps first, although not necessarily foremost, is the level of retirement funding. I think it is extremely wise when a person puts away an investment into his/her future through some form of savings, investment, or speculative plan, especially when it is their money that they are investing. I also see no problem in an employer contributing towards that retirement, because that contribution is really a wage, and a part of an agreement of employment. Now when this money is transferred to the employee, it comes from somewhere and the place it comes from within the private sector is out of sales revenue. Not necessarily from profits, but as an expense of doing business, and sales price of the employer product will reflect additional cost. In the marketplace, if the sales price of a specific product doesn't match the competitive price and the quality is no better, then this employer has a problem with staying in business and needs to find methods of reducing cost, improving quality, or else facing the consequences. However, in a monopolistic marketplace, and I would venture to place essentially all public sector products in that genre, the higher the cost of doing business, the higher the fee charged to compensate. Whadda life, huh? So make demands, and they will be met (at least until they "can't take it anymore").

Second, take a look at illegal immigration, something I have discussed earlier, and it is a major influence on the economy. I will simply reiterate my position that in addition to the basic flaunting of domain responsibility, two main factors come into play. Because the persons are here illegally, they cannot suitably contribute to the support of required government services through the system of taxation, they therefore will work for less cost (in many instances, their gross wage does not include taxes) and so will displace citizen workers, but they also take advantage of services that should be available only to the citizenry and accepted non-citizens. Enough said.

Well third, how about health-care, recently a really big issue due to the direction towards socialized medicine which is now a campaign issue and a platform issue. In the free marketplace- purchase whatever insurance is available that satisfies your needs, and that goes from no coverage to full cradle to grave coverage- all it costs is your money. But in the currently proposed version of the market, and under the auspices of what is termed "Obamacare", your choice is taken away-not only from whether to participate or not, not only whether you pay or not, but also in terms of what coverage you will get.

And fourth, let's just look at regulation of businesses. I am talking here about financial institutions, energy management, health care management, others. I will offer that in the free market system "nothing ventured, nothing gained" is a rallying call. It has issues though, and those relate to moral standards being balanced against personnel desires. Putting together national strategies is an intelligent thing to do, and is within the charter given to elected officials. Big BUT, premises have always been that these strategies are to lie within the guidelines set by the country's mission statement which really means protection of the rights and liberties of the citizenry.

SOCIALISM: of course such a system can work (the question is how well, and compared to what), because it is simply the establishment of a giant pool of contributors and users. It is a leveler, and so long as people are willing to be leveled, then there is no issue. But, are people willing to live in situations wherein essentially everything is contributed to the larger whole and then redistributed "according to need", resulting in a flat financial structure that is built to prevent stratification of any sort, even of ability? Of course, a second issue will become how much government intrusion is appropriate into the marketplace- should it be control or competition, or the elimination of competition in favor of big brother?

My definitions may fall technically short of full societal description, but hopefully you get the idea. Now comes a really tough part, and that is to develop meaningful comparative data that will allow whatever is the shining winner to appear. Usually, such a matrix is product related, and in this trade, although that is still true, the product being evaluated is societal structure, and so somehow the development needs to include human satisfaction as well as simply cold, hard, facts. My methodology of establishing values for the parameters will be using estimates and WAG's if appropriate, since detailed evaluation may improve the numbers, but I intuitively believe they will not change the values very much.

The matrix will look at the standard parameters for decision-making: COST, PERFORMANCE, SCHEDULE SUPPORTABILITY, RISK.

COST - Presentation of cost data for each of these societal models. It seems to me that the easiest way of base-lining would be to look at average personal income and ascertain how much discretionary spending remains from it for the use of each of us. I will focus on the individual citizen, not corporate entities, in terms of remaining discretionary income. Also, if you remember, the federal government currently spends on itself for services-rendered $34,000/household, but only collects $18,000/household.

Restoration- this model would place government as the only non-discretionary recipient of funds, in other words, those functions truly seen as falling within the charter of a duly established government per the requirements established within the Constitution. Utilizing the concept of a flat tax on income, and closing all loop-holes so that persons and corporations are seen in the same light, and offering the same services to all, ESTIMATE A CONSERVATIVE 20% OF INCOME TO RUN NECESSARY GOVERNMENT FUNCTIONS (this estimate is relative to today's AS-IS economy).

As-is- here we have quite a hodge-podge, and we must recognize that there are four main aspects to taxation roles. The first is the sliding scale of tax rates. The second is the differences between individuals and corporations. The third is tax loopholes. The fourth unfortunately is the continuing increase in the national debt. Additionally, the current role of government supplied entitlements is significantly higher than the bare essentials of supplying constitutionally created functions. **THE AVERAGE TAX RATE IS 35% OF INCOME**.

Socialism- oh my goodness, this one is pretty easy. It comes down to a very simple thing, how much will the traffic bear? I will simply estimate that almost everything can be government supplied if that is ukased, and on that basis, I WILL SAY THAT 80% OF INCOME COULD EASILY BE TAXED FOR THE COFFERS OF THE BIG DADDY ORGANIZATION.

PERFORMANCE-

This portion is not a "bang-for-the-buck" evaluation, simply a look at two things, what you get and how much is of your choice. Things will be examined in terms of free market product availability and choice of subscription.

Restoration- Well, you know the premise of this one, and that is that you get what you pay for. Because so many things have happened between its purity and where we are now, there needs to be a really careful look at what may be undone if we follow the letter of the premise. Even if we just establish that life, liberty, and the pursuit of happiness are the requirements that our government needs to assure, we have one heck of a big task to accomplish. All aspects of society need to be impressed by the "government mini-universal can opener"- "does this fall within the charter of government service per the constitution?", and if not, then free enterprise will fill the void with competitive products.
The "law" becomes the bottom line as to answers: protection of life, liberty, and the pursuit of happiness are the only criteria for government function. So let's see, once again we need an executive branch to implement the laws of the land, a judicial system to insure that only the laws are being applied and applied correctly, and then a legislative branch to deal with the sub-elements necessary to support the constitutional mission. That then leaves everything else to the free enterprise system. Here the biggest issue is to assure adequate competition so that some combination (of the least expensive and highest quality products of any line of endeavor) is available to the market place. Where government relates is to assure that competition remains open, that product line is not prevented, that market regulation and control does not occur either through government control or producer control. Products obviously are diversified, and a gamut of options would be

placed up for consumption, varying from the austere functionality to the gold-plated master whiz-bang. The marketplace will determine survival level through demand and supply-adjustment.

Of course, in a perfect world, this means an extremely wide range of product offerings, and if there is no collusion on the part of producers, then the full range will meet everyone's needs. For example, in the case of health care availability (not health care insurance!!!) policies would be available offering minimum coverage such as catastrophic, and with extremely high deductibles to assure that only catastrophe is eligible, thus keeping the cost of this coverage at an actuarially determined rate.

There is a big issue regarding pre-existing conditions, and again this needs actuarial rate determination. Here there would be no deductible since the specific condition's medical requirements would be known, and here the incentive would have to be for the health care provider to support the research necessary to reduce care-required expenses either through break-through resolution of condition or reduction in necessary care requirement. The balance would need to be established to charge the consumer the proportionately correct amount and to have some of the company's overall profit taken across to the research arena for investigative analysis and test.

All in all, the split of government versus private sector tasking would maximize the availability of consumer choices, and therefore result in a high level of satisfaction. In the return to true capitalism, premising that there is a need/job for every talent, then issues would not exist, and everyone would gravitate towards their goals and ideals. Thus in a rating scale, recognizing that there is a bell shaped curve of some sort for establishing percentage of citizen happiness, I would look at this concept of capitalism and say that as many as 90% of people would be satisfied if they truly got my implemented premises. THIS PUTS 10% AS DIS-SATISFIED.

AS-IS: This one is most interesting, because as-is is in a state of flux. There are obvious short-falls in today's system, as witnessed by the amazingly opposing positions of the platforms of our two major political parties, such an ideological split that the country itself is extremely divided, incensed, and polarized. From a "performance" point of view, from the perspective of the average citizen, we have a mixed and therefore adversarial set of appreciations. Each and every item discussed within the body of this missive shows the divergence of opinions, and demonstrates the unfortunate split in thinking and appreciation. I would have to say that at this time, we are probably dealing with 50-50 split in terms of feelings, but in terms of actual satisfaction, it seems that very few people are really happy with their current lot within the framework of today's economic society. So surprisingly, I would take the 50-50 split and call it opinion, but in reality say that less than 25% of the people would really be happy with things as they are, either due to cost or availability. THIS PUTS 75% AS DIS-SATISFIED.

SOCIALISM: The definition I provided above puts everything in perspective. The premise is that all things are reduced to least common denominator, that everything is flat, and that everyone has enough to exist. Beyond simple existence, there would be the requirement that everyone produce more, and that would raise the minimum standards. But that means envy and desire, and that moves away from the basic premise. So I must conclude that there will certainly be some portion of the bell curve that will be satisfied, but there will be a very large portion that must be dis-satisfied because the definition only provides the minimum. I would estimate that maybe 10% would be in the happiness regime, the rest would have to be looking at trying for improvement. THIS PUTS 90% AS DIS-SATISFIED.

SCHEDULE - to implementation:

RESTORATION: There is a lot of effort that would need to go into two main areas, the undoing of that portion that is not fully capitalistic and has placed undo charter on government services, and the build-up of the capability of the marketplace to truly and rightfully fulfill the needs of the consumer. Laws need undoing, institutions need establishment, the job market needs adjusting. Transition once again is the key, and the time frame MUST be long to get it right, because free enterprise and a free market economy are based on cyclical correction of errors. To allow for the normal marketplace correction, there must be at least 10 years to establish the first level and another 10 for first corrections, thus REQUIRING 20 YEARS FOR THE EXPERIMENT TO WORK.

AS-IS: man, this one is easy, just let it be. Of course, the issue is very simple, nothing will stay is as, forces will induce and require change, but at this time, all that can be said is that as-is means just that, AND SO THERE IS NO TIMETABLE, ZERO TIME REQUIRED FOR IMPLEMENTATION.

SOCIALISM: this will also be an experiment, but the implementation is easier than free market capitalism, because although there will be corrections, they all come from the governing source and so become law of the land with ease. A TIMETABLE FOR IMPLEMENTATION WOULD BE ROUGHLY 10 YEARS.

SUPPORTABILITY -

This is where we get into the consequences of the implementation of the various solutions, where we see what it takes to maintain our society based on its new definition. Support in this case will be defined in a vein similar to cost; it is the amount of a citizen's paycheck that will be allocated to maintaining the system, not the cost of using the system.

RESTORATION: Holy smokes Batman; there really is no cost to a return to a free enterprise system. All the costs of implementation will be borne by the private entities that either exist or will come into existence to support the needs that have been turned back to the market place instead of the government. Although initially the transition may impose some aspect of pass-through cost to the consumer, eventually it will stabilize to a final level. The dismantling of the government intrusions, the removal of the government oversight bureaucracy, and the movement of public sector employees into the private sector will be a one-time expense, but essentially a transition cost, not long term sustainment costs. One of the nice things about this approach is that more jobs will be created as the diversity and availability of services and goods increases. I would premise that taxation will reduce as we move to a fee-based free enterprise capitalistic system, and that the maintenance of the private enterprise system becomes embodied in the service fees, and definitely would not exceed the AS-IS of today. Looking at today and taking that into consideration, a purer free-market would not need more than 8% of the expected 20% cost to support the system.

AS-IS: we got what we got, and as I've said, I expect change and that depends on the platform of the elected party. So as of this writing, this definition of society will be base-lined as a reference. Premise 20% of the current 35% cost is associated with supporting the system.

SOCIALISM: one could argue that a single-payer system would have to be cheaper because there is essentially one system. BUT, recognize that now the single-payer government will be making all the decisions once made by individual citizens. A brand new bureaucracy will be instituted to run, police, and decide, on any and all services and any disputes. Notice that competition cannot exist in a SINGLE-PAYER system, so quality will be in the eyes of the bureaucracy, with little or no recourse for unhappiness. Not only will quality no longer be an issue, but cost will essentially be a matter of taxation rather than efficiency. Yes sir, gentle fall into decadence. Here we have a large increase in sustainment cost, because now service is premised as being required by all, the cost of supporting the system will be borne by all, the size of the administrative portion of the system has increased, and the staffing of the various service entities must increase as well. Of the expected 80% cost of the taxation for running the system, I would estimate that 35% would be required simply to maintain the system.

RISK - this item looks at the concerns of achieving an implementation that would be satisfactory to the definitions of the three systems. In each case, it is required to define the steps necessary to overcome any uncovered risks.

RESTORATION: there is always risk in a free enterprise system, the risk that any business will fail, and for various reasons such as: mismanagement, under-capitalization, poor product, poor advertising, poor staffing, and many more that could place the company into bankruptcy. But what the heck, this happens all the time. Not only that, but today's AS-IS is indeed the perfect model that shows the successes and failures and offers guidelines for the transition. I do not believe there is any risk to implementation.

AS-IS: obviously no risk to being what it is, the risk is the challenge of remaining as-is in such a dynamic political environment.

SOCIALISM: again, little risk of not achieving this end if that is the direction of choice. The only possible issue is the eventual recognition that the system may not be as defined in terms of achieving a utopian outlook.

So in terms of risk I would not place any of these choices as being in danger of not being achievable; however there could be possible dis-satisfaction with any of them, as is the lot of man.

MATRIX OF SOCIETAL ALTERNATIVES

SOCIETAL STRUCTURE ➡ PARAMETER ↘	RESTORATION	AS-IS	SOCIALISM
COST (% of personal income) taken for _non-discretionary_ spending	20%	35%	80%
PERFORMANCE **(dis-satisfaction)**	10%	75%	90%
SCHEDULE (years to achieve)	20	0	10
SUPPORTABILITY(% associated with maintaining services)-this amount is already a part of cost	8%	20%	35%
RISK (against achieving the societal definition)	None	None	None
TOTAL VIEW (Cost-support) =personal expense for societal services	ONLY 12% of personal income is used to maintain societal services	ONLY 15% of personal income is used to maintain societal services	A WHOPPING 45% of personal income is used to maintain societal services

CONCLUSION: No surprise, **Restoration** to a full free enterprise system offers the best bang for the buck. It suggests that when your money is spent by YOU, it will find best usage. The estimated 20 year period for implementation is based on the premise that getting it right is really not easy, and slow but sure wins the race.

You will notice that although today's "as is" has a value for what I call "total view" (your personal expense out of pocket for using the services) similar to full up "restoration", "Restoration" results in total cost to you being significantly lower (20% vs. 35%) because of your reduced support costs to keep the system going. All very logical and to be expected. What it says is that free enterprise will surely support the recovery of our economy, and provide each citizen with significantly more freedom of action and choice.

We need a plan for implementation to the "Restoration Alternative- Free Market System", a plan that does not overlook any of the elements discussed within this study; it is this plan that will do two extremely important things: it will rejuvenate the economy, and it will restore pride in self and country.

PISMO
ICE PLANT
PATH JEG
2012

FOURTH INTERLUDE
- AT PISMO

THE BEGINNINGS OF THE PLAN

ACTION 4- DEVELOP AN IMPLEMENTATION PLAN FOR RESTORATION OF THE FREE ENTERPRISE SYSTEM

First step is to re-assemble all the focus points that have been discussed, in order to create the elements of the plan. That means to go back and look at all the chapters of this package, look at the recommended plan for the society, and to pull things all together into a comprehensive implementation scenario. We've got a good start on this, what with my previous flow diagram of the economy that essentially takes each chapter and lines it up under an appropriate category. In the interest of simplicity, I have repeated the flow chart, because each of its pieces needs to feed into the solution's action plan.

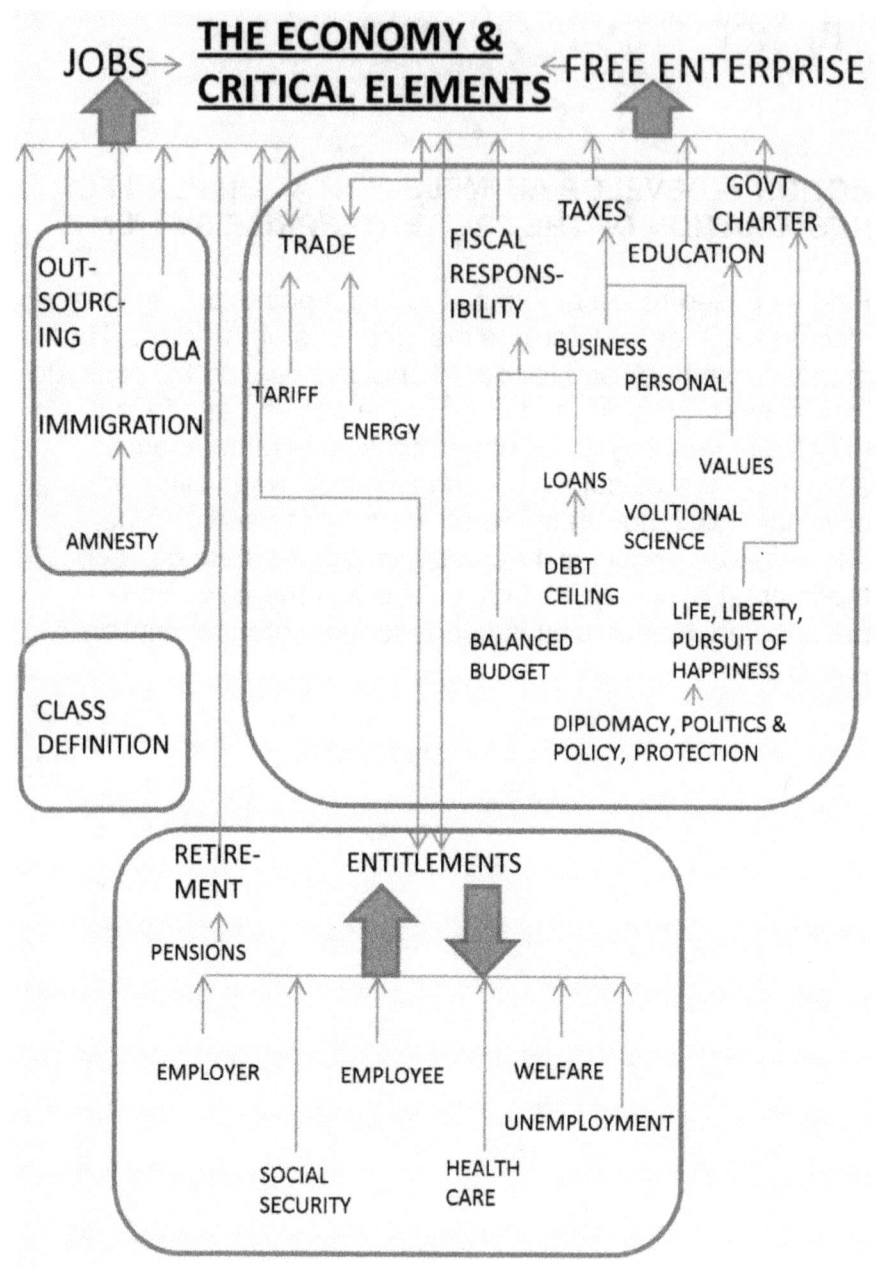

What I see as a break-out of all the pieces of the puzzle are four main areas that need to be addressed. The plan logically breaks down into a four pronged set of action activities, developed based on the flow chart "The Economy and Critical Elements". The subject matter of the flow charts will be rearranged as necessary to flow into the appropriate set of actions. These groupings are (not necessarily in order of importance):
1. Government Charter
2. Societal Classes
3. Illegal Workforce
4. Entitlements

The first thing to assure is that in any effort to *change* an active function, there will be a corresponding and deliberately established replacement of necessary functionality, to insure continuity. (For example, employment of qualified and necessary personnel in selected areas may be shifted to a more efficient operation.)

I will examine each of these areas to first establish goals, and then identify both problems and resolutions, with focus on the rather obvious areas that will not only improve operations, but most clearly provide a firmer handle on the element.

I MUST STRESS, THAT I AM ONLY FOCUSSED ON ACTIONS THAT DEAL WITH IMPROVING THE ECONOMY.

A TOP LEVEL LOOK AT THE LOGIC AND THE PLAN

Before I lay out the details of the plan and the actions necessary to carry it out, I will weave the elements together into a coherent whole that presents the overall approach.

The first thing to look at is what government has as a definition of purpose, which means that everything about government must remain strictly focused on the protection of the rights of free citizens, these rights deriving from the US Constitution.

This melds with the recognition that although we ostensibly live in a stratified society, it is really one in which any citizen can aspire to any goal, and that the ability to reach that goal will be protected by government, a government that protects any lawful individually motivated action instituted to satisfy the needs of any citizen(s). That occurs because of the imbedded requirement of respect for property, both physical and intellectual, as a part of the system. Government must promote such individualism by supporting a free market system, thus government is here for the purpose of protecting the common rights of citizenship.

The word "illegal" and its ramifications are critical to this plan, because government was formed to create the framework for protection of citizen rights, and illegal activity flaunts these rights. That means that contribution to society through legal and approved means such as voter approved taxation, and the need to take the illegality out of the equation, is critical. Illegal workforce must be identified and directed to recognition of obligation and becoming legal, and illegal immigrants need to be identified and action taken to resolve by either removal or to develop a legal path insuring that the immigrant becomes a contributor to the support of the government. Having taken such action, then certain jobs will be brought into the umbrella of legality as well. This will make more jobs available to currently unemployed citizens. Additionally, careful short term consideration of tariffs will allow US industry the opportunity to recover and improve the economy by creating new jobs.

Lastly, entitlements need careful review, because these are elements that require everyone's forced support, in many instances, for persons that have not suitably contributed or are not legally eligible. This therefore requires careful review of eligibility for certain programs, time span for eligibility, and a path to recovery out of the entitlement regime. This review must also show that in fact there is a requirement for the function, and demonstrate that the concept of insurance, purchased through the open marketplace, can satisfy all elements that entitlement professes to support, and as a purchasable rather than a give-away commodity, meaning that subsidy is not required. Again, transition is the key, and will provide a smooth implementation that will be careful to maintain promises already made as well as move into a different environment.

I am going to add that each and every aspect of the proposed plan is focusing on the basic problem of improving the economy and that the actions described are typically above and beyond the existing detailed activity of government. What is presented is designed to modify current perception of charter and to substitute with the proposals developed within this manuscript.

When it is all put together, this plan will foster business growth, improve the economy, create new jobs, promote an appreciation of property, and increase pride of self in all people.
Can you ask for anything more?

THE PLAN

GOVERNMENT CHARTER

Mission Statement: **Assurance of maintaining the charter of our government is a key element in maintaining the health of our country and its economy.** Government is instituted as a result of consensus between parties, that certain functions are best supported by a group chartered and dedicated to common cause, rather than by the individual. In these United States of America, the country was established through the Declaration of Independence, and the rules and guidelines of government by the US Constitution.
Government charter is established by the Constitution, which can be succinctly defined as protecting the rights of the citizenry to life, liberty, and the pursuit of happiness.
Government's function with regard to the operations of free market capitalism is to allow individuals and corporations to blossom as the market will support, to allow personal and managerial skills to determine how they rise and operate, to assure the protection of citizen rights, (and not be part of free market competition nor control of the free market).
Amongst the functions of the government are fiscal responsibility of the nation, protection of the citizen and property, and the development of policies consistent with government charter affecting citizens and interactions with other nations.

Objective: It is the requirement of this effort to insure that the functions of the government of the United States of America satisfy and remain within charter. This will act as a baseline for all subsequent actions and tasking.

Values: The country was founded on the principles of freedom of choice and assurance of protecting citizen's rights to life, liberty and the pursuit of happiness.

Premises:
> 1-The principles of our constitution remain valid; it is strictly the interpretation and application that comes into question.

Actions:
1. Assemble team, assign responsibilities, assign charter, confirm schedule
2. Elements and Guidelines
   a. FISCAL
      i. Budget:
         1. Institute requirement within budget process for submittal of estimates for 1, 3, 5 years, which will provide jump start on timely fiscal preparation.
         2. Balanced, on-schedule budget submittals.
         3. To provide incentive for compliance for submittal of a timely and balanced budget, penalties will be assessed against committee assignees incapable of meeting submittal requirements.
         4. A system of firewalls is to be established to compartmentalize funding and prevent unapproved shifts.
         5. Develop insurance alternative as a method of providing contingency services.

      ii. Loans/Bonds:

              1. Payback funding sources, schedules, and commitments to be delineated prior to bond issue.
              2. Cumulative commitments must not exceed solvency.
              3. Bail-out and bankruptcy rules to be improved and eligibility requirements to be delineated. Within the private sector, the concept of bail-out requires that prior insurance options be in place.

      iii. Debt Ceilings:
              1. Short term limits for potential budget over-runs require identification of repayment funding sources and timeframe.
              2. No consecutive increases without retiring prior over-run and reducing actual ceiling value back to nominal.

      iv. Taxes: (For both personal and corporation.)
              1. Flat income tax with no loopholes.
              2. Review and establish charter of income sources (taxation vs. fee) for various government functions.

      v. COLA:
              1. Phase out future use. (Each increment applied cheapens the overall worth of the dollar)

b. EDUCATION (the foundation for an intelligent citizenry)- consider both state and national purviews:
    i. Values:
              1. Requirement for curriculum content on the subjects of moral, ethical, and historical values to be instituted at grade levels. (Such values are the basis of the

foundation of this country; that successful effort leads to reward.)
2. Examine education and testing standards, teaching techniques, evaluation methods, teacher merit system, tenure definitions-(to improve level and worth of the curriculum).
ii. Volitional Science:
1. Requirement for curriculum containing the concepts and teachings of Volitional Science (as a method to imbed respect for property and worth).

c. POLICY
i. Basics (all United States policy activity has certain aspects of similarity that require boundaries). This includes:
1. Control of requirements creep
2. Establishment of timelines for transitional introduction
3. Consideration of non-partisanship
4. Assurance of individual choice
5. Stay within charter
ii. Energy:
1. Establish plan and action for United States energy independence to insure freedom of action and economic health.
2. Various energy sources to be explored, with proposed programs and recommendations prepared.
3. Establish consistent environmental requirements to be imposed on a transitional basis without exceptions, allowing that technology is always improving and that this legislation will be an

impetus to research as well as implementation.

   iii. Domestic:
1. Requirements for all policy to center on assurance of protection of all citizens' rights to life, liberty, and the pursuit of happiness without infringement on the rights of others.
2. Recognition that majorities and minorities have equal rights under the law, thus simple majority rule is inadequate to represent all conditions
3. Requirement for policy to foster free enterprise, maximizing the private sector (business-friendly/capitalistic) and minimizing the public sector.
4. Support incentivized programs channeled through education and entrepreneurship within the free-enterprise system to insure a full complement of jobs and workers competent in the job requirement.

   iv. Tariffs:
1. (In recognition of the need for time for transition in satisfying goals for improvement of the economy,) institute a finite time period of tariffs with a phase-in and phase-out framework.
2. (Such tariffs are not for the protection of indigenous activity, but are to promote the establishment and growth of such industry by focusing on the foreign labor aspect and bringing industry back to the United States.)

v. Fiscal/Budget:
1. Insure US triple A credit rating fiscal policy.
2. Contain and then reduce the national debt.
3. Minimize taxation.
4. Institute procedures to achieve balance and foresight in government spending per fiscal policy.
5. Institute lessons-learned from past system breakdowns to prevent recurrence.
6. Create viable funding sources, balanced accounting, submitted on schedule
7. Insure provision that crisis control will allow doing what is necessary to recover, with the stipulation that a recovery plan is mandatory to eventually obviate the need for this crisis management.

vi. Diplomacy/Foreign:
1. Promote US interests as a primary goal.
2. Promote world interests in fallout from US interest.
3. Trade interfaces and agreements must recognize a finite world market.
4. Cost/benefit analysis supporting agreement choices to recognize moral requirements, and must benefit US society.
5. Diplomatic agreement is a contract which must be honored.
6. International trade must have a moral component, and is a factor in relationships. (Political special

interests and lobbying cannot trump standards of conduct.)

SOCIETAL CLASSES

Mission Statement: The premise of society in the United States of America has always been that there are no restrictions of access to any level of society, both private and business. What becomes the prerequisite to personal improvement in a moral society is that personal determination, drive, knowledge, interfacing, and hard work are the factors that will determine how high or to what level a person may move. There are many facets to the make-up of society, including business, financial position, ethnicity, religion, race, social involvement, and location. Ethnicity, race, and religion are factors typically established at birth and are sometimes viewed with a different perspective than the others. **It is necessary that equality of opportunity remain the governing criteria for place and advancement within the societal system of the United States. From the economic side, perspective must be the goal of achievement, rather than the goal of maximized dole.**

Objective: It is one of the goals of this effort to guide the focus of our society towards this full equality of opportunity, and to insure that citizen assets are maximized to improve the health of the society.

Values: Class is a misnomer; breadth of condition is the appropriate terminology. All citizens provide their capabilities to the marketplace, the marketplace allows for natural sorting of personnel, talent, and compensation. The move from position anywhere within the workplace and/or society is based strictly on the effort expended to achieve.

Premises:
1. The free marketplace establishes the avenue of achievement
2. Desire for achievement is established by each individual

Actions:
1. Assemble team, assign responsibilities, assign charter, confirm schedule
2. Elements and Guidelines
   a. Concept of 99%-1%:
      i. Government continues to insure free discussion of ideas under freedom of speech.
      ii. Government to insure that educational lynchpins promote self-worth and the ability to offer skill-sets to the marketplace free and independent from any coercive activity. Government speaks for all citizens.
      iii. Government to ensure equal access to opportunity in the workplace.
   b. Majority/Minority: cross-sections of the citizen population are drawn according to an almost unlimited number of categories. These include race, religion, geographic location, ethnicity, wealth, political inclination, sex, sexual preference, marital status, employment, housing, age... Since government must represent all with an equal voice, it is noted that simple majority is inadequate for many decisions.
      i. Establish a decision code that recognizes minority as well as majority interests.
   c. Private/Public Sectors: Competition is the byword of the private sector while access to taxpayer funds is the source of public sector finance.

      i. Perform study identifying and offering corrective action if public sector activity overlaps the realm of private enterprise, bearing in mind the limitations of government's charter.

  d. Equality of Opportunity:
      i. Insure that individual choice is maintained for private sector purchases, for work choices.
      ii. Insure that no subsidies or laws require change to the dynamics of the free market.
      iii. Develop planning with private industry to increase availability of private funding for education.

ILLEGAL WORKFORCE

Mission Statement: Illegal workforce is an umbrella that encompasses illegal status as well as illegal operation. **The law of the land which defines both worker requirements and worker contribution to the country is clear and the enforcement of such laws is clear.** "Law of the Land" premises that citizens and those with granted special status will operate within and abide by said law. Illegal immigration which brings foreign nationals within the bounds of this country without permission, and illegal workforce, which allows workers outside the normal support for this country's institutional requirements, are both a direct cause of financial shortfall within the system.

Objective: It is the intent of this segment to review the aspects of illegality, define corrections, and offer a plan for resolution. Focus will be on jobs, outsourcing, and entitlements.

Values:
1. The law of the land must prevail.
2. Law-breakers will be brought to task.

Premises:
1. Methods of citizen identification are in place

Actions:
1. Assemble team, assign responsibilities, assign charter, confirm schedule
2. Elements and Guidelines:
   a. Immigration Laws:
      i. Develop a clear, firm, consistent, enforceable definition of legal/illegal immigration.
      ii. Develop federal laws and methods establishing activity that can identify status of persons within the boundaries of the United States.
      iii. Establish, delineate, and differentiate, federal and state levels of jurisdiction with regard to illegal workforce.
      iv. Define and implement border integrity.
      v. Establish "grand-father" considerations for selected categories of illegal entrants, including legal status through issuance of appropriate card of status. Re-examination/confirmation of Constitutional assurance of citizenship for those born in the United States
   b. Immigrant Workforce:
      i. Existing Green Card status to remain.
      ii. Establish worker card status as identification and system recognition.

          iii. Pay levels to be established by the marketplace. Pay subject to normal taxation rates.

c. Amnesty:
          i. Develop Worker card for specified qualified persons, with specified benefits and reporting requirements.
          ii. Develop system for status, eligibility, and penalty evaluation of prior time without legal status. Visitor status to the qualified, allowing raising those children grand-fathered in.

d. Outsourcing: This is a sign of a world economy. At this time, the premise of this study effort has been to recognize that the economy of the United States, being influenced by but independent of any other country, is in the throes of a very slow recovery (no matter what is happening elsewhere).
          i. On that basis, and to assist in this recovery, it becomes necessary to transitionally insulate portions of the economy to allow for draconian control and a more rapid recovery. Two aspects of outsourcing will be placed under the auspices of control.
               1. Study to define eligible areas for creation of temporary programs regarding outsourcing relative to insularity.
               2. Establish tariff to be imposed on selected sub-contracted merchandise.
               3. Establish company penalty for outsourcing without necessary and sufficient cause.

e. Illegal Work Contracts: this aspect deals with under the table contracts, either between company and customer, company and employee, individual and employee. This is a practice that results in deliberate violation of the lawful financial taxation requirement between company/person/government.

    i. Establish sufficient audit capability of tax returns, or lack of return will identify the illegal practice.

    ii. Tax laws require improvement to resolve this issue. By requiring workers to properly register, full visibility will result.

    iii. Establish methodology for determination of illegal work contracts in process.

ENTITLEMENTS

Mission Statement: The concept of insurance defines certain provisional plans for eventualities. Through this concept have sprung up ideas and programs to cover such areas as

-Retirement through auspices of social security, pensions, and retirement savings plans

-Welfare through recognition of certain criteria regarding minimum supportable income for select individuals

-Health Care through consideration of financial and other eligibility for medical needs

-Unemployment through recognition of the sometimes transitory nature of work requirements

The concept of insurance in a free market would allow choice in selection of type of coverage for each eventuality.

However, seguing into the concept of entitlements offers an entirely different perspective, one which subtly replaces "provisional" with "required". At that point what was originally choice has become mandate, both on the receiving end as well as the giving end.   And the giving end no longer involves choice, it involves ukase. The shift involves replacing the free enterprise marketplace, capitalistic system with a socialistic structure, the purpose of which is income redistribution in the name of "fairness".

Consistent with the values of this country, citizen life should be based on self-sufficient capability, including the planning necessary for the future.

Objective:
1. Identify and eliminate trends and programs that have focused on replacing the free enterprise system with a demand/socialistic system.
2. Encourage activity to ensure minimum cost availability of free enterprise options for citizen's selections.

Premises:
1. The marketplace will assure that qualified and suitably registered persons have access to a range of established available alternatives.
2. Eligibility requires citizenship or appropriate legally defined non-citizenship.

Values:
1. An individual's right to choose to use or support these services is a free market/free enterprise choice
2. Current systems burden the individual's work value through redistribution of wealth
3. For these services, charity is an acceptable form of giving, taxation is beyond the constitutionally established charter of government, fee is a choice, and insurance is a choice.

Actions:
1. Assemble team, assign responsibilities, assign charter, confirm schedule
2. Elements and Guidelines

a. Funding Review: Review current financing of the services through taxation, charity, insurance options, fee options, resulting in matrix of alternatives and recommendations.
b. Social Security-
    i. Create consideration of transitional replacement with self-imposed savings plan or insurance option.
    ii. Review economic benefits of:
        1. Tax increase
        2. Revised retirement age
        3. Elimination of COLA
        4. Reduced benefits
    iii. Current system can be phased out but requires revised formula of both contribution and age-eligibility during its phase-out period.
    iv. Since social security is a retirement program, dove-tail with actions below considering retirement options.
c. Welfare-
    i. Require work-reward program implementation.
    ii. Establish responsibility clauses for both fathers and mothers, to stop abuses of the system.
    iii. Establish appropriate time-limits for eligibility.
d. HealthCare-
    i. Establish required range of free-market insurance choices, with gamut of available services.
    ii. Establish free marketplace choice of subscription.
e. Unemployment-
    i. Insurance to be funded from while-working salary.
    ii. Short term benefits.
    iii. Labor pool for job availability.

   iv. Continuous validation of solvency of the system.
     1. Recovery plans for non-solvency possibility
 f. Retirement-
   i. Define choice of cash now or benefit later.
   ii. Allow transfer of benefits from job to job, from donor to beneficiary.
   iii. Establish insurance concept as an option for investment, such as modified annuities.
   iv. Pension funds must show solvency calculations and risk/reward analysis as well as funding and funding source profiles.

PROGRAM PLAN AND SCHEDULE

I have prepared a program schedule based on the plan above. This schedule offers a quick look at the main topics of the plan and provides a guideline for implementation. I think a schedule is critical to an effort, because even if it is wrong, once the stakeholders are involved, it will amazingly become modified and the committed persons will strive to maintain or improve it.

The entire program is exciting, because it is the tool to steer the entire nation back on-track. To be a part of this program means that you are validating your commitment, dedication, and belief in our wonderful United States of America, and have become a vocal and positive force in strengthening not only our heritage, but the future of your children and their children. The text of this manuscript lays out some basics for development, the program plan pulls all these loose elements into a cohesive all, one that can be visualized and established as a step-by-step forward-moving entity. The schedule, as I have mentioned, is a straw man, deliberately a placeholder, as a first attempt at an implementation. I expect that as commitment grows, the content of the plan and the timing of the schedule will be improved. I also know that I have put together only the framework of a working plan, and rely on the thought processes of the assignees to un-jumble my program plan and make it their own, and to move it into implementation.
God bless, and please, enjoy.

Joe Goldstein

ID	Project Name	Nature of Task	Months	Start	End	Q1/Q2	Q3/Q4	Q5/Q6	Q7/Q8	Q9/Q10	Q11/Q12	Q13/Q14	Q15/Q16
	US RECOVERY PLAN		48	Jan-15	Dec-18								
1	GOVERNMENT CHARTER		36	Jan-15	Dec-17								
1.1	Fiscal		30	Jan-15	Jun-17								
1.1.1	Budget	Balanced, Timely	27	Jan-15	Mar-17								
1.1.2	Loans/Bonds	Repay funs ID'd	12	Oct-15	Sep-16								
1.1.3	Ceilings	Close-out timely	12	Oct-15	Sep-16								
1.1.4	Taxes	Graduated vs Flat	36	Jan-15	Dec-17								
1.1.4.1	Personal		36	Jan-15	Dec-17								
1.1.4.2	Corporate		36	Jan-15	Dec-17								
1.1.5	Cola	Not Acceptable	12	Oct-15	Sep-16								
1.2	Education		36	Jan-15	Dec-17								
1.2.1	Values	Part of curricula	24	Jan-15	Dec-16								
1.2.2	Volitional Science	Part of curricula	27	Jan-15	Mar-17								
1.3	Policy		36	Jan-15	Dec-17								
1.3.1	Basic Policy Guidelines	Overall rules	6	Jan-15	Jun-15								
1.3.2	Energy	environmental	27	Jan-15	Mar-17								
1.3.3	Domestic	Citizen Awareness	27	Jan-15	Mar-17								
1.3.4	Tariffs	Transitional Need	15	Oct-15	Dec-16								
1.3.5	Fiscal/Budget	Credit Rating, Protedtion	18	Jan-15	Jun-16								
1.3.6	Diplomacy/Foreign	US Interests	30	Jan-15	Jun-17								
2	SOCIETAL CLASSES		27	Jan-15	Mar-17								
2.1	Concept of 99%---1%	Equal Oportunity	18	Jan-15	Jun-16								
2.2	Majority/Minority	Full citizen cross-section	18	Jan-15	Jun-16								
2.3	Private/Public Sector	Competition	18	Jan-15	Jun-16								
2.4	Equal Opportunity	Choices Available	18	Jan-15	Jun-16								
3	ILLEGAL WORKFORCE		36	Jan-15	Dec-17								
3.1	Elements and Guidelines	Overall rules	6	Jan-15	Jun-15								
3.2	Immigration Laws	Integrity	27	Jan-15	Mar-17								
3.3	Immigrant Workforce	Worker Card	27	Jan-15	Mar-17								
3.4	Amnesty	Worker Status	24	Jan-15	Dec-16								
3.5	Outsourcing	Transitional Penalty	24	Jan-15	Dec-16								
3.6	Illegal Work Contracts	High Penalties	18	Jan-15	Jun-16								
4	ENTITLEMENTS		36	Jan-15	Dec-17								
4.1	Funding review	Sources	6	Jan-15	Jun-15								
4.1	Social Security	Savings Plan	27	Jan-15	Mar-17								
4.2	Welfare	Work/reward	27	Jan-15	Mar-17								
4.3	Health Care	Market Choices	27	Jan-15	Mar-17								
4.4	Unemployment	Insurance	18	Jan-15	Jun-16								
4.5	Retirement	Self-Insrance	18	Jan-15	Jun-16								
5	REPORTING	Quarterly Reports	45	Jan-15	Sep-18								
6	FINAL REPORT	Conclusions, Recommendations	24	Jan-17	Dec-18								

Note: all program elements allow first month for personnel formation

Note: color denotes report prep by group

PROGRAM PLAN AND SCHEDULE

A FOND "AND WHAT'S NEXT"

Well gang, I've somewhat exhausted myself on this one. I have put together some pretty rough ideas based on the way I see the economy and the way I would approach improvement. Nothing perfect, but it's a plan, so waddya think? Please tear it apart if that is your inclination, I am happy to accept criticism, because after all, I am just one pre-conditioned mind seeing things in my own pre-conditioned way. But most of all, and most importantly, I am trying to elicit some action other than the current stale-mated political process that fears to move forward because it might stumble against some antipathy or some vitriolic spoutings or some downright angry feelings. Well and good, because as I said, it's time to get off the pot. The status quo in which we are now embroiled is a lousy mess. The "gimmes" are rotting the basic pillars of our society, and what we are finding is less and less pride in self, less and less pride in accomplishment. So what's next? Simple. Get off the pot. Embrace your own feelings and your aspirations, and see if there is something of worth within this manuscript, something you can adjust to your own satisfaction and then embrace as your own.

And for heaven's sake, do it with gusto, and why not do it now?

ACKNOWLEDGEMENTS

This book is a derivative of what I prepared in my first book, "Things of Concern". However, in this case, acknowledgements are strange, because the impetus and drive for the book's preparation has been what I see of the current political and social status of this country. My conversations with friends and acquaintances have shown me that the mood of some of the country has changed; either due to complete apathy, a feeling that even though things are not right there is very little that can be done about it, that educational background offered through our universities has shifted tendencies, or lastly that this shift is a right thing to do no matter what.

But equally, I would also like to acknowledge all the forms of threat to the free world and its open free economy- those zealots, terrorists, and tyrants who would squelch the growth of the individual spirit reaching for freedom and expression.

To me, third world status for the United States, in internal domestic policy and in foreign relations, is not alright. The United States is a hallmark and bastion of individualism and capitalism, and its current status in the world is a shining light against the onslaught of tyranny.

And so, I would like to acknowledge that my conversations with friends and family have been the strongest of incentives, that conditions have been a major factor as well, and all have required that I put my own thinking in order so that I could clearly delineate my positions, and come up with a path forward. That path includes the restoration of our economy to its full potential.

To the Reader,
This is my second book, the first one concerned with the overall inter-relations of man within the universal perspective of civilization. Hopefully, that book will have some impact on the way people deal with other.
This book is focused on how the make-up of the society of the United States of America is so critically influencing the country's economics (and vice versa). I am not sure which is the cart and which is the horse, but as I see it, the boot-strapping momentum of our economic make-up is creating one "heck-of-a-mess". I went through quite a lot of mental turmoil as I tried to pin-point any one main source of this decay, and instead, I came to realize that everything related. And so my theme, and so my title. Once corralled, the causes readily came together into an amalgam that was both identifiable and lending of itself to rectification. And so my book. Enjoy.

Joe

Joe Goldstein was born in 1938 in New York City and currently resides in Los Angeles, California with his wife Donna. He worked in aerospace for 42 years, with specialties in analysis, system engineering, and project management. Amongst his passions is sensitivity to the sanctity of personal property.

www.ingramcontent.com/pod-product-compliance
Lightning Source LLC
Chambersburg PA
CBHW072309290526
45794CB00002B/586